Sex, Sacrifice, Shame, and Smiting

SEX, SACRIFICE, SHAME, & SMITING

IS THE BIBLE ALWAYS RIGHT?

DONALD KRAUS

SEABURY BOOKS
New York

Unless otherwise noted, biblical quotations herein are from the New Revised
Standard Version Bible translation, copyright © 1989 by the Division of Christian
Education of the National Council of the Churches of Christ in the U.S.A. Used by
permission. All rights reserved.

Other biblical quotations are noted as follows:

Robert Alter, *The Five Books of Moses: A Translation with Commentary* (New York:
W.W. Norton & Company, 2004).

NASB: *The New American Standard Bible.* Copyright © 1960, 1962, 1963, 1968,
1971, 1972, 1973, 1975, 1977, 1995 by The Lockman Foundation. A Corporation
Not for Profit, La Habra, California. Used by permission. All rights reserved.

NIV: *The Holy Bible, New International Version®.* Copyright © 1973, 1978, 1984 by
the International Bible Society. Used by permission of Zondervan Publishing
House. All rights reserved.

RSV: The Revised Standard Version of the Bible, Old Testament section, copyright
1952; New Testament section, first edition, copyright 1946; second edition,
copyright 1971; the Apocrypha, copyright 1957; the Third and Fourth Books of
the Maccabees and Psalm 151, copyright 1977 by the Division of Christian
Education of the National Council of the Churches of Christ in the U.S.A. Used
by permission.

Tanakh: *Jewish Publication Society Tanakh* translation. Copyright © 1985, 1999 by
the Jewish Publication Society. All rights reserved.

Library of Congress Cataloging-in-Publication Data

Kraus, Donald.
Sex, sacrifice, shame and smiting: is the Bible always right? / Donald Kraus.
    p.   cm.
Includes bibliographical references.
ISBN 978-1-59627-068-8 (pbk.)
1. Bible—Criticism, interpretation, etc. 2. Bible—Evidences, authority, etc. I. Title.
II. Title: Sacrifice, shame and smiting.
BS511.3.K73 2008
220.1—dc22

                                                    2008027155

Cover design by Jennifer Glosser / 2Pug Design
Interior design by Vicki K. Black

Printed in the United States of America.

Seabury Books
445 Fifth Avenue
New York, New York 10016
www.seaburybooks.com

An imprint of Church Publishing Incorporated

5   4   3   2   1

CONTENTS

PREFACE

WHEN THE REVEREND Gene Robinson was elected the Bishop of New Hampshire in 2003, the rector of the parish where I was then a member—the Reverend Douglas Fisher at Grace Church, Millbrook, New York—asked if I would lead a discussion about the difficult passages in the Bible dealing with homosexuality. I agreed to do this only if we could look at these passages in a larger context: that of biblical texts dealing with money, social justice, and other difficult issues; texts that seemed to endorse violence, vengefulness, or prejudice; and texts that were extremely radical in their political and economic requirements. Only then, I thought, could we look at the specific passages dealing with same-gender relationships in a way that would allow us to open them up in a far different context than that of their original audiences. This book, with considerable additional material, is based on those sessions, and I want to thank Father Fisher and the people of Grace Church for their helpful responses to my first efforts to make these issues clear.

Many people, when they read this book, will first look at the chapter on homosexuality. There is nothing wrong with starting there, but if that is the only chapter they read, they will not be able to grasp the full import of the argument of the book as a whole. That argument is that the Bible presents us with many difficult passages, and we need to have a way of dealing with all of the problematic texts, and not simply choose those that are in keeping with our existing biases or political or social leanings. Confronting texts that make us nervous, that challenge us, or that (implicitly or explicitly) judge us is never a comfortable activity, but it is necessary if we are ever to learn to have a mature response to the Bible as a whole.

In writing this book I have been helped immeasurably by continuing conversations with my wife, the Reverend Doctor Susan Kraus. Our faiths and theologies have grown together, to the extent that it is now impossible for me to separate my ideas from her ideas and from our ideas. I owe her more than I can ever say in both intellectual and emotional wisdom.

Cynthia Shattuck, my talented and creative editor, has made this book what it is. Her able revisions and her insistence on keeping in mind the audience of the local Christian community, for whom it is intended, have made it a sharper, more focused, and (I hope) more readable book than it would have been had I been left to my own resources.

The Reverend Deacon Vicki Black has prepared the book for the press with her usual attention to detail and her experience of parish work and education. I thank her for the care with which she has approached this book, as she has approached every project.

Finally, I dedicate this book to all those people, famous or nameless, who have suffered marginalization at the hands of those who call themselves Christian: the Jews, the women, the members of other racial groups than the dominant ones, and especially those—some of whom were themselves extraordinary Christians—who are my gay and lesbian brothers and sisters. Whoever you are, wherever you lived, your witness for integrity and for the worth of every human being should stand as an inspiration to all of us. I thank you and honor you with a full and humble heart.

LOOKING FOR GUIDANCE

Does the Bible Always Help?

The Bible is the Manual for Living, Life's User Guide, the spiritual diet for the believer....
> — *Lesson 11, The Bible Course*
> *Stewarton Bible School, Scotland*

The Word of God . . . is full of interest. It has noble poetry in it; and some clever fables; and some blood-drenched history; and some good morals; and a wealth of obscenity; and upwards of a thousand lies.
> — *Mark Twain, Letter III of "Letters from the Earth"*

THE BIBLE MOST CERTAINLY has the power to pro-duce contradictory opinions in those who read it—or even in those who do not. Mark Twain's "Satan," the purported author of the "Letters from the Earth"—writings that were considered so scandalous that they were never published in Twain's lifetime, or for fifty years afterward—presents Twain the unbeliever's view of the Bible as a primitive hodgepodge of poetry, morals, and barbaric thought. The Stewarton Bible School, on the other hand, maintains a widely held characterization of the Bible as God's manual for human life and behavior.

Twain's opinion of the Bible, that of a humorist and satirist who had been exposed in his youth to forms of Protestant piety that he rejected, remains that of the nineteenth-century skeptic. For such a mind, perhaps understandably given the cultural dominance in America of a Protestant civic religion, there was really no third choice aside from the alternatives of unthinking credulity and thinking agnosticism. The present-day view of many Christians, that the Bible is both a sacred text and a human artifact that must be read critically, was simply not an available opinion for the ordinary reader in Twain's time.

The Stewarton view, prevalent though it is in some circles— I have heard sermons essentially making the same point, one with a direct analogy between the Bible and an operating manual for a power lawnmower—raises problems in the opposite direction. To take only the most obvious: if God is the author of the Bible and intends it to be the manual of life for the believing Christian, could it not have been written a little more clearly? We are all very familiar with the experience of buying a new electronic device and then discovering that the operating instructions for it are unclear and confusing, but there at least we understand that these instructions are written by other human beings, and that being able to design an electronic device is a different skill from that of being able to write clearly. But the Bible has no such excuse: God (presumably) can do anything, including write clearly. People sometimes point to the Ten Commandments as providing the basis for living. But aside from the fact that the Ten Commandments are very unrepresentative of the Bible, they are also incomplete: they make no mention, for example, of charitable deeds, which most people would wish to include among the rules for living a good life; in addition, they are addressed (as we will note below) exclusively to males. If you depended only on the Ten Commandments for your moral rule book, you could logically conclude that while men may not covet their neighbors' wives, women are perfectly free to covet their neighbors' husbands.

Clearly, we will have to take a somewhat different view if we are going to make sense of the Bible's varied rules and its apparent moral strictures. This is all the more important when we are engaged, as we now are in a number of different Christian denominations (and in Judaism as well), in arguments about where moral guidance can be found and what moral behavior is. The Bible can be a valuable help here, but it is not the sort of help that will automatically provide answers, like some kind of ethics cash machine, if you just put in the right codes. It is more like consulting widely among friends, many of whom have differences of opinion among themselves, and trying to come to a decision based on all the advice and insight that you can gather. And first, we must look at the actuality of "the Bible" itself.

The Bible is a varied collection of writings, put together in various places and by various groups of people over the course of more than a thousand years. Partly as a result of that process of development, in places it can be complex and hard to understand. For people of faith, obscure passages can be a challenge, but also an opportunity for deepening our understanding. Wrestling with thoughts that are difficult to grasp can be a kind of mental exercise, similar to competing with a better chess or tennis player. It can build "muscle" and agility, and help us think or react more quickly and accurately. More important, it can deepen our insight and widen our sympathy—both spiritual benefits we can all use more of. Some of the difficult passages in the Bible, therefore, though they may require effort in research or in reflection, clearly help bring about growth among those who accept the Bible as religiously authoritative. This is in keeping with what the Bible itself, in various passages, says. For instance, one writer praises the study of *torah* in Psalm 119.97: "Oh, how I love your *torah*! It is my meditation all day long." The New Testament author of 2 Timothy urges study of the "sacred writings," saying: "All scripture is inspired by God and is useful for teaching, for reproof, for correction, and for training in righteousness . . ." (3.16). In John's gospel, Jesus promises his followers, "I still have many things to say to you, but you cannot bear them now. When the Spirit of truth comes, he will guide you into all the truth" (16.12–13).

There is a different sort of difficulty in the biblical text, however, and it is a much more serious challenge to a mature, committed faith. What are we going to do with those Scripture passages where there seems to be little doubt what the Bible means to say, but what it means—about money or sex or justice or politics—is exactly where the difficulties begin? For one reason or another we may not want to accept what the Bible says. Sometimes we don't want to accept it at face value; sometimes we don't want to accept it at all. It may seem impossible, utterly impractical, unwise (or downright foolish), immoral, or just plain wrong.

Despite the common opinion that such difficulties with the Bible are a purely modern phenomenon primarily afflicting those at the "liberal" end of the spectrum of believers, these kinds of difficulties affect all of us, and have for many centuries. Conservatives as well as liberals, and ancient writers as well as contemporaries, have all encountered passages that seemed to threaten their faith, but they dealt with them nevertheless.

These problems are those of the believer, however, and not the scholarly commentator. For the author of a scholarly commentary on Exodus, for example, there are difficulties to be solved—authorship, date, obscure vocabulary—but how the text is to be applied to one's life or how it might help to solve some ethical quandary is not among them. A scholar, writing as an historian or literary critic, would see the Bible as a collection of writings, an anthology, assembled over the course of a millennium or more. Clearly principles of selection were at work— some writings were included, others were excluded—but these principles are not entirely clear, and what's more, there are different "selections" for different groups. There are books that everyone agrees on (Genesis, Psalms, Isaiah) and others (Sirach, Judith) that only some include, and, of course, Jews do not accept the New Testament at all.

All of these considerations, and many others, mean that for a scholar *as a scholar* the Bible does not have to be internally consistent, nor does it necessarily have to apply to present-day life. A scholar can belong to a particular religion, but his or her scholarship, if it is to have scholarly integrity, must not favor it. If a passage in a biblical text creates difficulties in the modern mind, there is no scholarly need to reconcile the passage with contemporary moral norms. And if one biblical passage seems to contradict another, that is no reason not to regard both as equally authentic—or inauthentic—since "authenticity" in this context means only that some recognized group has accepted the passage as part of the Bible.

For those who accept the Bible's authority in any sense, however, the situation is quite different. If passages in the Bible seem to be making a demand—stating a moral imperative, endorsing or denouncing a social arrangement—and that demand is impossible, or wrong in any way, then we need to have some principles on which we can base our objections. If passages in the Bible seem to be in conflict, we must have intelligible reasons for preferring one to the other, or for reconciling them so that we can try to understand the Bible's underlying point, or for putting them in a wider context that makes clear that each is a partial view of a larger truth.

As we work our way through various biblical passages that challenge our moral sense, our practical knowledge, our understanding of the world, and our own experience, we should try to keep in mind how to read these passages with the fullest sense of the biblical context we can muster. In the following pages we will look at texts that are violent, texts that demand extremely challenging economic behavior, texts that seem to advocate unacceptable political and social arrangements, and texts that, perhaps, overly regulate and restrict sexual behavior. In each case, we will be confronted with a text that some or all of us would not wish to honor without adjusting it to our understanding—or, in some cases, would not wish to honor at all. In our examination of these texts we will try to develop ways of reading them that offer principles of interpretation that can allow us to keep faith both with the Bible and with our understanding of the way things are. There will be texts that challenge conservative approaches, and there will be texts that confront liberal understandings.

For many of those who have taken positions on progressive issues, such as the ordination of gay and lesbian candidates in committed same-sex relationships, it is frustrating when those on the other side of the issue continually accuse them of abandoning the Bible. That is not really the case. Nor is it true that two different methods of reading the Bible are in conflict, although that is also frequently charged. Instead, what is at issue is a difference about which parts of the Bible to emphasize, and whether strictures about sexual behavior—specifically, homosexual intercourse—are at the same level of importance as doctrines about God, teachings about social justice, or efforts to reach out to marginalized persons of all sorts so that all may hear the good news of salvation. Neither side is "abandoning" the Bible, but each side has firm ideas of what the Bible says and why.

The point is not to bring to the Bible all of our assumptions and prejudices in order to find support for them in the text, or to discard the text when it conflicts with something we already think. But neither is the point to find out what the Bible says, or seems to say, and simply apply that to how we live our lives. Things are never that easy. In addition, no one—*no one*—agrees with everything that the Bible says we should be doing, or refraining from. (If you don't believe me, read on. I guarantee that there will be plenty of moral imperatives from the Bible that you would have nothing to do with.)

The issue, then, is not that we should never interpret the Bible in such a way as to temper its demands, or even put them aside in favor of better understandings derived from elsewhere. That has always been done, and will be done, by people of all theological persuasions. The issue rather is to be honest—honest with ourselves, and honest with each other—about what we are doing and why. If someone wants to put aside biblical strictures on poverty and economic behavior because (he claims) we now know more about how economies work and can judge the impracticality of trying to live by biblical rules, that is all right. We may even agree with a proponent of "democratic capitalism" that the Bible, with its communitarian ethics and view of the world as God's possession rather than ours, is naïve or simply wrong. But we can then ask such a proponent of a specific nonbiblical economic view why we cannot apply an equally keen analysis, based on current knowledge, to the Bible's psychological understandings and sexual rules.

So the decision about which verses to apply to our lives, and how to apply them, is not an easy one to make. We sometimes hear from people about a specific verse or passage dealing with one topic that "you can't just take verses out of context and apply them." That is true in a narrow sense, but it is true in a broader sense as well. The "context" of a verse, for someone who believes that the Bible is meant to guide us into truth, is the entire Bible itself. We must remember that in our experience of any great and complex work of art—a landscape, a symphony, an epic poem—comprehension and enjoyment are not simply a matter of noticing details and individual passages, but of seeing how one detail or passage modifies another to produce the overall effect. The brushwork, the harmonies, the imagery and metaphors do not exist for themselves alone, but rather in service to building up a whole complex unity.

So it is with the Bible. Each verse or passage of the Bible is, at least potentially, in dialogue with every other verse or passage. Until that dialogue takes place, we may not fully understand what a particular section of the Bible is telling us, or how we should apply it. And, in trying to understand how we might apply one passage of the Bible to one kind of situation, we may be able to discover principles of interpretation, adjustment, and modification that can apply to other passages dealing with other situations as well.

That at least is my hope. The actual application of any given passage is up to the individual reader. I have my views on various topics, and they will become plain—I have thought it best to put all my cards face up. But I hope that I will also accomplish two things. One is to present enough of the biblical text so that others with differing presuppositions can come to conclusions different from the ones I have come to. In other words, I hope to have provided the materials necessary for arguing against me as well as agreeing with me. The second aim, and one I have tried very hard to keep in view as I have put this book together, is to bring myself—and my readers—to be more careful about claiming "what the Bible says" without taking into account nuance or context. We all need to learn to be more cautious. I believe firmly in dogmatic theology: I accept as a basic article of faith, for example, that "God is love" (1 John 4.8). Dogma, for me, is the indispensable floor or foundation on which we all move, and the basis on which we each can build a house of faith. I find less helpful a notion of dogma that sees it as a set of walls, or closed doors, designed to keep some people inside and the rest outside. Dogma must be in some sense definite, in the sense of "defined": that is, we should be able to articulate our beliefs at least to the extent that someone else can understand them. But it is sadly the case that too many people seem to confuse being definitive with being exclusive. We all stand on the same ground; if we can't all live in the same house, we can at least refrain from condemning houses we ourselves don't want to live in. As Matthew's gospel tells us (7.24–27), it is the foundation of the house that is supposed to be made of stone rather than sand; the nature of the house itself is not described.

Rules and Regulations
In reading the Bible's moral rules and exhortations, Christians often make a distinction between those rules that have to do with such matters as dress and diet—rules that are deemed to have been suspended by Jesus and eliminated for Christians by the arguments of Paul and the actions of the early church—and those that deal with strictly moral matters. When we actually begin to look at the Bible's rules, however, we find quite an array of specific regulations, some dealing with particular situations but also more general applications, and we may find that we cannot so easily separate the purely moral ones from those having to do with arbitrary matters such as dietary restrictions. To take just one example, the command "You shall love your neighbor as yourself" (Leviticus 19.18) occurs just before "You shall not let your animals breed with a different kind; you shall not sow

your field with two kinds of seed; nor shall you put on a garment made of two different materials" (Leviticus 19.19). Note that this last command would preclude the breeding of mules (the result of mating a male donkey and a female horse) and the production of clothing made of linen and wool ("linsey woolsey" was a common clothing material on the American frontier) or cotton and polyester (which is the cloth used to make many shirts and blouses today). And, unlike Jesus' abrogation of food regulations ("Thus he declared all foods clean," [Mark 7.19]), these "mixture" regulations were never explicitly repealed. But the larger point is that the command to love one's neighbor, given its placement in the text, is not differentiated in any way from the commands that follow it, although most people would recognize it as on an entirely different moral level than strictures about animal breeding, agricultural practice, and cloth manufacture.

Many other regulations fall into a gray area, and it would be difficult to classify them in the category of kosher food laws, distinctive clothing, and other practices of Judaism from which Christians are presumably exempt. On the other hand, though they deal with matters of behavior or are otherwise intended to promote morality, they are not the kinds of regulations that we would be likely to carry out today.

For example, here is a regulation about the punishment to be imposed in a particular situation:

> If men get into a fight with one another, and the wife of one
> intervenes to rescue her husband from the grip of his
> opponent by reaching out and seizing his genitals, you shall
> cut off her hand; show no pity. (Deuteronomy 25.11–12)

The issue here is not whether this situation is likely to arise, but rather what we should do about rules such as this. Penal codes in Western countries no longer contain punishments like cutting off hands, and it is unlikely that any will resume such penalties in the future. Nevertheless, here in the Bible is a specific case, treating a situation which is not intrinsically impossible, yet there is no general effort on the part of Christians to make sure that such a penalty is available to be imposed. Why not?

Here is another rule, dealing with a situation which is, unfortunately, all too common:

> If there is a young woman, a virgin already engaged to be married, and a man meets her in the town and lies with her, you shall bring both of them to the gate of that town and stone them to death, the young woman because she did not cry for help in the town and the man because he violated his neighbor's wife. . . .
>
> But if a man meets the engaged woman in the open country, and the man seizes her and lies with her, then only the man who lay with her shall die. You shall do nothing to the young woman; the young woman has not committed an offense punishable by death. . . . Since he found her in the open country, the engaged woman may have cried for help, but there was no one to rescue her.
>
> If a man meets a virgin who is not engaged, and seizes her and lies with her, and they are caught in the act, the man who lay with her shall give fifty shekels of silver to the young woman's father, and she shall become his wife. Because he violated her he shall not be permitted to divorce her as long as he lives. (Deuteronomy 22.23–29)

As the context makes clear, these rules deal with forcible rape, since part of the issue is whether the woman cries for help. They have nothing to do with consensual sexual intercourse. So it is troubling that in the case of the virgin who is not yet engaged to marry someone, the penalty for the rapist is that he will pay a bride-price to the young woman's father (who is regarded as the one chiefly injured) and will be forced to marry the woman. The consequence of this, of course, is that she also will be forced to marry her rapist with no possibility of ever being separated from him except by his death. To my knowledge, no Western government has instituted this rule as a penalty for rape, and there is no Christian effort to get such a law on the books. Yet here it is, in the Bible. Why is there no movement to enshrine this rule in our laws?

In the United States, as we all know, our political system is partly based on a clear separation between church and state. Does that mean that we are exempted from trying to get such laws on the books? If so, then those who are opposed to equal rights for homosexual persons could not argue—as many do—that the strictures against homosexual behavior that are in the Bible are part of their motivation in arguing against legal efforts to legitimize civil rights, including marriage, for gay and lesbian people. But, though I disagree with such people, I think they have every right to argue as they do. Separation of church and state means that the state cannot promote a particular religion; it does not mean that religious people cannot, by political action, try to enshrine in our legal system laws that represent what they think of as moral behavior. My argument with such people is different: if they think that the (very few) passages in the Bible about homosexual behavior mandate that Christians try to make our legal system express a particular approach to homosexuality, why are they not trying to get our legal system to reflect other aspects of biblical law? Why pull out a couple of regulations about homosexuality, and ignore other laws about caring for the poor?

Here is another example of a penalty to be imposed in the case of a specific behavior:

> If someone has a stubborn and rebellious son who will not
> obey his father and mother, who does not heed them when
> they discipline him, then his father and his mother shall take
> hold of him and bring him out to the elders of his town at
> the gate of that place. They shall say to the elders of his town,
> "This son of ours is stubborn and rebellious. He will not obey
> us. He is a glutton and a drunkard." Then all the men of the
> town shall stone him to death. So you shall purge the evil
> from your midst; and all Israel will hear, and be afraid.
> (Deuteronomy 21.18–21)

Apparently a disobedient, gluttonous, drunken son should simply be put to death. So the Bible says. Yet there is no organized effort to get such a law on the books in any jurisdiction. Why not?

It is possible to argue about these cases in the following way. "We have advanced beyond where the authors of the biblical texts were in our understandings of moral behavior and, particularly, in our understandings of punishments. We no longer, in Western countries, think that severing limbs is an appropriate form of punishment. We understand the trauma that rape causes, and we would not force any woman to marry her rapist in order to keep to the understanding that once a woman has lost her virginity, she is 'damaged goods' and not a fit object of marriage for any other man. And we would not impose the death penalty for such minor infractions as disobedience, gluttony, or drunkenness."

It is possible to argue in this way, but it opens a very dangerous door for those who are bent on using the Bible as the only moral measuring rod. Once we argue that our moral thinking has advanced beyond that of biblical times in one area, is there anything to stop us from arguing this in many other areas as well? We cannot arbitrarily take this line of argument in some cases, but disallow it in others.

Sin, Shame, Purity, and Sacrifice
There are still other parts of the Bible that may not cause disagreement but that are completely foreign to our experience and can therefore be misleading. These are not areas in which the Bible is wrong so much as those in which we can be misled because our assumptions are very different. What we need to do, for our own benefit in reading the Bible, is to see if we can locate a core meaning or intention in these concepts that speaks to our present-day concerns.

For example, sin: most of us do not even want to hear about it. We think of lists of prohibitions, of people claiming others are "bad" because they don't like their behavior. It reminds us of the most unpleasant parts of childhood: "Don't do that!" But sin in the Bible is not quite the same thing. To be sure, there are prohibitions—"You shall not murder," for example (Exodus 20.13). Nevertheless, in both Hebrew and Greek the words for "sin"— *chattat* and *hamartia*—have root meanings that derive from missing a target or falling short of a goal. And that provides an essential clue to the biblical understanding of sin. The point is not an enumeration of "bad deeds" that we must avoid, though there are clearly things that we are not to do. More important, there are positive deeds, things that we clearly are meant to be doing, and not to do them constitutes sin.

Further, the matter of what to do and what not to do is a means to an end. What God wants from us is the attainment of something that is our proper goal: full humanity. And it is not just our own full humanity, but the help and support we will be giving to others in their own efforts. Of course, we may believe (I think, correctly) that the actual attainment of our full humanity is beyond our capacity. Striving toward our full humanity, however, is not. Calling on God's help in this effort is also part of our duty. Taking this approach to understanding sin is not an effort to let ourselves off the hook or to make things easier for us; it is ultimately far more demanding. But it does get us away from an understanding of our actions that breaks them up into discrete deeds that are judged individually, and instead allows us to look at our patterns of behavior to understand whether they are moving us toward the goals of fuller integration and greater humanity, or away from them. If we look at sin in this way, we will be better placed to understand what the Bible is saying about it.

In Romans 3.23, Paul makes the following statement: "for all have sinned and fall short of the glory of God" (NASB). Both words are interesting: "sinned," as noted, means "missed the target"; "fall short" here means literally "arrived late," in other words, "missed the opportunity." The word used here is derived from *hysteron* ("later"). It appears, for instance, in the parable of the prodigal (Luke 15.11–32): after the prodigal has spent his money, a famine arises in the land and "he began to be in need" (v. 14, NASB); literally, "he came late," or as we might say, "he came up short." Paul's meaning in this phrase is not so much that we have failed because we haven't obeyed God's commands, but rather that we have not attained our true nature because we have failed to grasp an opportunity. That opportunity is being offered to us again, along with the grace to work toward it: we are now "justified as a gift by His grace through the redemption which is in Christ Jesus" (Romans 3.24, NASB).

One brief passage in the Hebrew Bible also makes this very clear. It occurs in Proverbs, at the end of Wisdom's exhortation to all people to seek her out. She ends with the following statement:

> For he who finds me finds life
> And obtains favor from the LORD.
> But he who misses me [*chot'i*, "falls short of me,"]
>   destroys himself [*naphsho*, "his *nephesh*, his very life"];
> All who hate me love death. (8.35–36, Tanakh)

The point, therefore, is not primarily to do good deeds and avoid bad deeds; that is part of wisdom but certainly not the whole of it. Rather the point is to align ourselves with the basic structure of the created universe: as Wisdom remarks earlier in this passage, regarding her role in the creation of the universe, "I was there when He set the heavens into place; . . . I was with Him as a confidant" (vv. 27, 30, Tanakh). To "miss" or sin, therefore, is to fail to find our proper place in the whole scheme of being, and therefore to be unable to fulfill our destiny.

Another category of thought in the Bible that is foreign to us today, at least in the Western world, is that of shame. Many societies in the ancient world, as well as some today, are organized around principles of honor and shame. In the Greco-Roman world particularly, "honor"—the true estimation of the worth of someone or something—is a very important part of the social fabric, and a failure to pay the honor due to someone is to cause them shame. This value system is sometimes exemplified and sometimes undermined in the New Testament.

The word generally translated "honor"—*time* (pronounced "tih-MAY")—means "valuing, according something its true worth." Thus in Matthew 13.46, the merchant of pearls finds one pearl of "great price" (*polytimon*) for which he trades everything else he has. The honor due to someone, therefore, is the correct assessment of their worthiness, their "true value" according to the estimation of those giving them honor. In Romans 13.7, for instance, Paul simply accepts the common understanding that we should "pay what we owe": "Give everyone what you owe him: If you owe taxes, pay taxes; if revenue, then revenue; if respect, then respect; if honor, then honor" (NIV).

In other passages, however, the understanding of honor in the wider society is undermined. In Paul's discussion of the Christian community as "the body of Christ" (1 Corinthians 12.12–31), among the points he makes is that the estimation of value within the body of Christ is not the same as that in the outside world: "The parts that we think are less honorable we treat with special honor" (v. 23, NIV). In other words, the Christian view is to accord more honor to those whom the world accords little or no value. This should not come as a surprise when we remember Jesus' words about the last and the first, those who will inherit the kingdom, and so on.

The opposite of honor is shame. The main New Testament word for shame (*aischros* and derivatives) means "base, dishonorable." What is dishonored is not accorded its true value; it is held in low esteem undeservedly. We must keep this cultural idea in mind when it comes to discussing such matters as shameful sexual behavior.

A third such biblical concept, that of purity, is a particularly difficult one for us to understand. (In many translations, the words "clean" and "unclean," rather than "pure" and "impure," are used. The underlying concepts are clearer, however, if "purity/impurity" is kept in mind. The distinction has nothing to do with hygiene; it is a matter of ritual acceptability.) Sources of impurity include: ejaculation of semen (Leviticus 15.16–18); menstruation (Leviticus 15.19–24); skin disease (Leviticus 13.1–46); and contact with carrion (Leviticus 11.29–40).

The remedy for all of these situations is the same: bathing oneself or washing one's clothing in water, and then waiting a set period of time (until sundown or for a given number of days), after which point the impurity is eliminated and the person can approach God in the Temple. Although we may be misled by the part of the ritual that involves bathing into thinking that physical cleanliness is at issue, the waiting period should alert us to the fact that this is a ritualized action.

What lies behind at least some of the purity rules is a concern that the person should not transgress a boundary that is part of God's order. The major boundary is that between life and death; crossing that boundary (which we all will do, but which God, being life and the source of life, does not) puts us unalterably in a different category from God, and therefore unable to approach God in worship. Situations in which we come too near that boundary—by loss of bodily fluids symbolizing life, like blood or semen; by succumbing to a skin disease that may be seen as death encroaching on our life; by touching something dead; and so on—render us unfit to approach God in an analogous way.

Although we cannot adopt these practices directly—indeed, except for purification bathing after menstruating, observant Jews do not carry these strictures out any longer—we can see them as aiming toward integrity or wholeness in the individual and the community as a means of drawing closer to God. The person or the community coming to God in worship is thereby encouraged to be honest about who and what they are. We know that we will never be able to attain absolute perfection, total personality integration, but we can strive to present ourselves to God in our worship as openly and honestly as we know how. Hiding things about ourselves, pretending to be something other than what we are, is not in accordance with this sense of the underlying meaning of the purity laws. Coming before God and recognizing the places where we have fallen short, and also the reality of where we are right now, is a part of true worship. This striving toward integrity is of great importance in our determination of what rules of life and behavior we will require from members of our congregations and from those who will lead those congregations as ordained persons.

Finally, in our consideration of biblical concepts that may cause difficulty for people in today's world, we need to look at the biblical practice of sacrifice. Israelite religion, like other religious systems in the ancient Near East and the Mediterranean, involved the sacrifice of animals as part of the worship of God.

Rules for such sacrifices are given, for instance, in chapters 3 through 7 of Leviticus. They involve both those sacrifices that are necessary if one wishes to eat meat and those to be carried out in the case of one's need to be cleansed of sin.

The actual practice of these sacrifices fell into disuse when the Second Temple was destroyed by the Romans in A.D. 70. Early Christians, however, still participated in the Temple worship (see, for instance, Acts 2.46); and although the letter to the Hebrews (in chapters 7 and 8) outlines how, in the view of the early Christian community, Jesus Christ's death on the cross stands in place of and perfects the Temple sacrifices, it still uses the thought forms and ideas of such sacrifice to make its point. And Christianity never explicitly renounced the Temple sacrifices; rather, as with Judaism, the destruction of the Temple and the consequent inability to carry out such sacrifices made the issue moot.

How can we appropriate this idea for our own use, since clearly we are not going to begin sacred slaughter in any of our churches? Sacrifice means "to make holy" (it is based on Latin roots, *sacer, sacri-,* "sacred" and *-ficere,* "to make"); the main Hebrew word for sacrifice, *zabach,* means "slaughter"; the Greek verb *thuo* means "offer"; the noun derived from it, *thusia,* means "offering." Thus to "make something holy," in the biblical context, is to offer it to God, the only intrinsically holy being. We can understand sacrifice, therefore, as giving, or giving back, something to God. The way in which something is given to God is to put it beyond our own use: to kill it, burn it, pour it on the ground, or chase it off into the wilderness. These are all ways in which something of value—livestock, fowl, wine, or grain—are offered to God. When something is dedicated or offered to God, it is treated in such a way that the one who is offering it cannot withdraw the gift.

Ultimately, of course, the sacrifice that we as Christians see as our model is that of Jesus Christ. We can therefore understand the crucifixion not as a tragic end but as the final expression of a human life lived not according to the person's own will and desire, but in complete submission to God, a continual offering on Jesus' part throughout his life. A human life lived according to the love of God is, in fact, in our world likely to bring the person into conflict with those who administer worldly power; thus Jesus' acceptance of his death, and his final submission to it, both validate and complete his willingness to live according to God's will, not his own.

These four concepts are, as mentioned, not a part of our everyday experience, but they do work together toward a vision of what the true human community is meant to be. We are meant to be striving toward our full humanity; to be treating ourselves and one another according to the worth that God has granted us; to be working toward being "all of a piece," integral beings both individually and corporately; and to be offering that fully human, honorable, and integrated personhood back to the God who has given it to us. Seen in this light, these biblical concepts are not foreign to our experience after all, but are directly relevant to our efforts to live our lives in full community with God and with one another.

How We Approach the Bible
As a last step before moving into problem areas of the biblical text, we should look briefly at a few issues that are not strictly speaking matters of the Bible itself, but rather of how we are going to approach the Bible for moral guidance. The first of these matters is what we might call the "countercultural argument": we should not look to our surrounding (presumably corrupt) culture for moral insight or guidance. Many of the people who were opposed to the ordination of women used this kind of argument to condemn it as part of a secular, radical feminist agenda that had no basis in the Bible or Christian tradition. The fact that nonreligious feminists were pressing for women's equality in various careers, such as law and medicine, became evidence that those who wanted to enable women to become ordained clergy in various denominations were serving this same secular, even godless, purpose.

The difficulty with this argument is that "outside cultural influences" have been a part of the biblical text and the development of Christian thought throughout their histories. Furthermore, movements such as those for religious liberty, democratic government, civil rights for minority group members, social welfare, and other progressive causes have had both religious and secular backing. To cite one clear biblical example, the Book of Proverbs 22.17–23.11 follows the content and order of an Egyptian collection of proverbs, "The Instruction of Amen-em-opet," which the author or compiler of Proverbs must have used in some form. There is simply no time in the history of the Bible, or in the development of Christian thought, when there was no influence from the wider culture.

The issue then becomes one of discerning when secular culture is promoting a moral insight that is worthy of adoption. Most of us now would agree that religious liberty—that is, the idea that each person should be free to practice whatever religion he or she chooses, or no religion at all—is the correct position to take, and that no outside power—a government, a state church, or anything else—should determine what anyone's religious affiliation or practice should be. This movement toward religious liberty was at least in part a secular one, joined by Christians for strategic reasons (if they were in the minority in a particular area, for instance). But in the sixteenth century almost everyone in Western Christianity believed the exact opposite: it was taken simply as a matter of course that the ruler in a particular area should have the right to enforce religious conformity on all who lived within its borders. In practice, of course, accommodations were made: powerful nobles in England were allowed to practice Roman Catholicism; Catholic religious practices were licensed for resident aliens—ambassadors, merchants—from Catholic countries. Protestant churches were allowed in Rome for the use of expatriates. But the principle was well-established that the religion of a particular area was what the ruler said it was. That is no longer the case, and any effort to reinstate such a practice would meet with strong resistance from Catholics and Protestants alike.

A second objection is what we might call "the argument from consensus." People sometimes make the following point: "It is true that we have abandoned certain practices that the Bible encourages (like polygamy) or permits (like slavery). But, to take slavery as a specific example, it took many centuries before Christians agreed to stop the practice, and this change happened only when there was a general consensus among Christians. It was not a minority view imposed by a few. That is the model that we must follow in making adjustments to the Bible's moral rules. When the vast majority of Christians have agreed to abandon a biblical practice (like slavery) or to ignore biblical prescriptions (like severing limbs as punishment), then we will know that it is the Spirit that is leading us to make the change."

Such a view ignores the actual process by which consensus is achieved. It does not spring up from nowhere. For important matters like the abolition of slavery, it almost always begins among a small group, even a tiny one. The fact is that the majority of the people in any situation are very unlikely to undertake a reevaluation of a moral determination. They only do so—and, usually, with great reluctance and much complaining—when the situation is forced on them by someone else's action. The white majority in the United States did not gradually agree to abandon slavery; it was forced to confront the practice by a relatively small group of abolitionists. A century after the Civil War, the white majority did not move to end racial segregation until a small group of African-American and white activists raised the issue and initiated specific political action. It is naïve to think that painful but necessary change will always happen by gradual (and painless) consensus.

More recently, the movement for women's ordination was not the result of a consensus slowly building among the majority of members in various denominations, but rather the result of smaller numbers who pressed for this change and in some cases forced it, as with the 1974 "irregular" ordinations of women in the Episcopal Church ratified by the 1976 General Convention. Though change by consensus is not impossible, it is certainly not the normal or usual route of change.

This does not mean that every view held by a minority of Christians is the correct view. It means, instead, that we cannot assess the moral worth of a view simply by looking at whether it is a majority or minority one. We must be willing to undertake a process of discernment about a given view regardless of how many, or how few, people hold that view.

Finally, there is what might be called "the Bible's finality" argument. This essentially states that the Bible itself shows development on those issues where moral thinking has advanced, and therefore we are secure in following the Bible where it demonstrates that moral advance is possible. We are not, however, on firm ground in advancing a moral argument where the Bible itself does not show any revision of a moral claim. Thus, for example, the abolition of slavery can be justified by looking at the biblical development of thought about slavery, which moved from rules about slavery in Exodus 21.1–6 to the letter of Philemon, in which Paul argues for treating a slave as a fellow-believer. But since both Israelite (Leviticus 18.22) and Christian (Romans 1.26–27) texts condemn homosexual practice, we cannot argue for taking a more progressive view of it.

This is, however, a very narrow way of looking at how the Bible teaches us. It would be just as logical to argue that the Bible has provided *some* examples of rethinking certain topics, slavery being one, so that we can see how moral argument can advance. Then we are left to make further applications ourselves. We have certainly done this with regard to women's rights, which are *not* held in high regard in the biblical text. With increasing understanding of human psychology and development, we may be able to make a case for an understanding of gay and lesbian relations that differs from the Bible's. There is at least a reasonable argument to be made, and we should consider it before trying to short-circuit the process simply by appealing to the Bible as it stands, without an understanding of the development of thought within the Christian tradition.

Whatever we may decide about the literal application of a particular text, however, we should always make the effort to try to derive some insight or application from even the most unpromising text. We can gain nothing by simply avoiding difficult texts. There is value in trying to get behind them, to see what the authors were trying to accomplish, and to wrestle with texts that challenge our assumptions. We will, naturally, find texts that we do not want to apply literally or directly; the question is whether we can, nevertheless, gain some spiritual insight or benefit even from those texts that we find most abhorrent.

And, more than simply not avoiding such texts, we should also refrain from prematurely dismissing or denigrating them. It is all too easy to label a text as "patriarchal" or "communitarian," as "utopian" or "homophobic," instead of doing the hard work of listening to it, trying to understand it in its context, and seeing whether there is anything in the text that can give us insight for today.

That is really the point of such an exercise. Within the wide reach of the Christian community, our differences on certain matters can seem so stark that we tend to concentrate not on discerning truth, but on refuting one another—and that includes refuting one another's favorite Bible passages. The polemic overwhelms the irenic. We are so busy trying to push other people out of our territory that we refuse to see that we are all standing on God's earth. Of course, in the end we may simply have to disagree on the most difficult subjects. But we can at least explain how we approach them, and make clear to those who disagree with us that we have reflected on these matters and are not simply dismissing them as unworthy of our attention. We can continue to listen to those with whom we disagree, remaining open to the possibility that we may come to understand something that we have missed hitherto. If one side or the other simply shuts down the conversation—refusing to listen to or engage with the other, simply repeating points without trying to understand an alternative point of view—then all understanding is potentially crippled. We can all work toward the goal of making sure that everyone is heard, but also that everyone listens.

VENGEANCE

Does the Bible Let Us Get Even?

"Go ahead, make my day."

— *Dirty Harry*

IN THE MOVIE *Sudden Impact,* Detective Inspector Harry Callahan of San Francisco (played by Clint Eastwood) confronts a villain holding a waitress hostage. When the villain threatens to kill his hostage, Harry responds with a classic line—"Go ahead, make my day"—that has joined "Round up the usual suspects" and "Frankly, my dear, I don't give a damn" in the pantheon of immortal movie quotations. Harry's implied threat—"Hurt her and you're only giving me an excuse to beat you to a pulp, blow you away, or worse, and I'd really enjoy doing that"—expresses the natural human desire to wreak vengeance on evildoers, even to excess. And, vicariously, at least, we can all join in with Harry and admit that "getting even" in certain circumstances might feel really good.

Taking one's revenge on someone, or wishing to do so, is natural. But is it right? The Bible seems uncertain. Some Scripture passages exhort us to refrain from taking vengeance; others celebrate the triumph over one's foes and urge the most grisly kind of retaliatory actions. Clearly when we look at some of the passages involved we will have to think very carefully about how they might apply to our lives and our actions toward those who may have injured us or those we love. Furthermore, in order to determine what we think the Bible means to teach us, we may have to downplay or reinterpret some passages and take a good look at other parts of the Bible where it may seem to be contradicting itself. We will certainly have to bring to bear our own experiences in real life, and do some deeper investigation of how some of the Bible's most difficult passages—which themselves are contradicted by other texts—may ultimately make much more sense in the real world than Dirty Harry does.

Vengeance Is Mine

"Vengeance is mine, I will repay, says the Lord" (Romans 12.19). The idea that vengeance is God's business and not ours may be a noble ideal and one to which we should aspire. It is so admirable that it is quoted twice in the New Testament: in Romans and in the letter to the Hebrews (10.30). Yet is this really what the Bible says about vengeance? Are we supposed to leave it all to God? What does this ideal in fact mean?

The original quotation is not from Romans, but from Deuteronomy 32.35. In the text of Deuteronomy, these words occur at the end of the farewell speech of Moses, before the Israelites enter the promised land. (Moses' death is related two chapters later, and the people enter the land under the leadership of Joshua.) Chapter 32 is the final section of Moses' speech, the "Song of Moses," a poetical ending to the entire book and his final testimony before his last blessings.

Deuteronomy itself is a complex and sophisticated composition, in which Moses summarizes the relations of Israel and God up to that point, and issues words of comfort and warning. The statement about vengeance is among his words of warning: it occurs in a passage in which Moses is partly speaking for himself and partly speaking on behalf of (or relating the words of) the LORD. The immediate passage begins with verse 19: "The LORD saw and was vexed and spurned His sons and His daughters" (32.19, Tanakh). At the point of the statement about vengeance, the passage continues:

> Ah! The vine for them is from Sodom,
> From the vineyards of Gomorrah;
> The grapes for them are poison,
> A bitter growth their clusters.
> Their wine is the venom of asps,
> The pitiless poison of vipers.
> Lo, I have put it all away,
> Sealed up in My storehouses,
> To be My vengeance and recompense,
> At the time that their foot falters.
> Yea, their day of disaster is near,
> And destiny rushes upon them.
>   (Deuteronomy 32.32–35, Tanakh)

In context, therefore, the line about vengeance (here translated "To be My vengeance and recompense"—or, as Robert Alter translates it, "Vengeance is mine, requital," which makes the point clearer) is that God will repay the people with the fruit of their faithlessness. Far from meaning, as is usually supposed, "Do not take it upon yourself to avenge injustice; God will right the wrongs, in the time that God judges best," the line actually means, "The consequences of your own iniquity and faithlessness will be the punishment visited on you when God acts to right the wrongs you have done."

Most Christians, however, remember the line from its uses in the New Testament, where its appearance is also instructive. In the letter to the Hebrews, the writer deals with the forgiveness of sin by means of the sacrificial death of Jesus and then goes on to point out the danger of continuing to sin after such forgiveness:

> For if we willfully persist in sin after having received the knowledge of the truth, there no longer remains a sacrifice for sins, but a fearful prospect of judgment, and a fury of fire that will consume the adversaries. . . . For we know the one who said, "Vengeance is mine, I will repay." And again, "The Lord will judge his people." It is a fearful thing to fall into the hands of the living God. (10.26–31)

Here the writer has grasped the intent of the passage from Deuteronomy: the warning that falling away from one's faithful adherence to God—into idolatry, sin, or apostasy—will bring out the vengeance of God. The words are far from comforting or peaceful.

But in his letter to the Romans, Paul takes the phrase as meaning what most people conventionally assume: that vengeance is God's task, not ours (12.14, 17–21):

> Bless those who persecute you; bless and do not curse
> them. . . . Do not repay anyone evil for evil. . . . Beloved, never
> avenge yourselves, but leave room for the wrath [of God]; for
> it is written, "Vengeance is mine, I will repay, says the Lord."
> No, "if your enemies are hungry, feed them; if they are thirsty,
> give them something to drink; for by doing this you will heap
> burning coals on their heads" [Proverbs 25.21–22]. Do not be
> overcome by evil, but overcome evil with good.

Paul here associates the injunction to renounce vengeance with Jesus' positive commands to love one's enemies and pray for one's persecutors (Matthew 5.44).

Here is a good example of the Bible seeming to contradict itself—for here, as we see from both the passage in Deuteronomy and its use in the letter to the Hebrews, Paul is misreading Deuteronomy. This is more than creative exegesis on Paul's part; he is making the words mean something very different from their original intent. Does this misreading matter? We will return to this point after a brief look at some places in the Bible where, it would seem, we are stirred up to avenge ourselves, or at least to rejoice when vengeance falls on others.

Vengeance Is Ours?

Few books of the Bible are as well-loved, or as often quoted, as the Book of Psalms. For those who read the Psalms regularly, as part of a prayer discipline or meditation, there are many gemlike passages that seem always to reflect and refract the light in new ways. Down through the centuries, people have found courage and consolation in many places in the Psalms; as one example, let us look at Psalm 137.1–6 (RSV).

> By the waters of Babylon,
>   there we sat down and wept,
> when we remembered Zion.
> On the willows there
>   we hung up our lyres.
> For there our captors
>   required of us songs,
> and our tormentors, mirth, saying,
>   "Sing us one of the songs of Zion!"
>
> How shall we sing the Lord's song
>   in a foreign land?
> If I forget you, O Jerusalem,
>   let my right hand wither!
> Let my tongue cleave to the roof of my mouth,
>   if I do not remember you,
> if I do not set Jerusalem
>   above my highest joy!

The bitter poignancy of this lament still speaks with almost unabated fervor after twenty-five centuries. The Temple singers, who have been exiled by the Babylonian invasion from their city and their Temple, weep to remember those former days. The singers cannot bring themselves to sing, and they set aside their instruments. In the midst of their pain comes the crowning touch: their jailers, their exilers, *demand* that they sing—and sing *happily*—for the entertainment of those who have caused them the greatest sorrow of their lives. The psalm then moves to a personal reflection that anyone who has suffered a grievous loss can understand: I have suffered, but worse than suffering would be to forget what I have lost. Do not let me forget! Inflict further pain on me if ever I forget—if ever I fail to honor what I have lost as the highest thing I have ever known!

It is a beautiful psalm, and it grabs you by the throat. Its embodiment of mourning for loss has echoed through the centuries since, summed up in one of poetry's greatest expressions of anguish: "How shall we sing the LORD's song in a foreign land?" There has never been a more perfect evocation of the pain of exile.

Often omitted from this psalm, however, especially when it is used in worship, are the last three verses. It is these verses that we should therefore read closely, to find out *why* they would be omitted.

> Remember, O LORD, against the Edomites
> > the day of Jerusalem,
> how they said, "Rase it, rase it!
> > Down to its foundations!"
> O daughter of Babylon, you devastator!
> Happy shall be he who requites you
> > with what you have done to us!
> *Happy shall be he who takes your little ones*
> > *and dashes them against the rock!*
> > > (137.7–9, RSV, emphasis added)

What lies behind this terrible cry of vengeance? The Edomites, according to the prophet Obadiah (vv. 8–14), stood by and watched as the Babylonians invaded and destroyed Jerusalem, gloating over its fall and grabbing loot when opportunity arose. They even blocked the escape routes and pointed out to the invading army where those who were escaping might be going, and caught some of the survivors and turned them over to the invaders themselves. Worse, of course, were the Babylonians themselves, who—as the psalm says—deserve to have done to them what they did to others. That they were brutal in their invasion we can have no doubt; war is always brutal, and ancient war, being a matter of direct confrontation rather than death at a distance, relied on the blood-lust of its soldiers to succeed in an invasion of an enemy city.

The last verse, "Happy shall he be who takes your little ones . . . ," could better be translated, "Happy *is* he who takes" or (following the New Jewish Publication Society *Tanakh*), "A blessing on him who. . . ." The same phrasing as used here occurs in Psalm 146.5: "Happy is he whose help is the God of Jacob."

"Happy" is meant not just subjectively, as in "This person feels happy," but objectively: "This person is in a good situation." The point of the statement in Psalm 137 is that it is, and would be, a commendable thing to grab up a Babylonian baby and smash its brains out against a rock. God, and others, would approve.

How are we to read this verse? It is unambiguous, a bare assertion: this act of vengeance is not wrong and to be condemned; it isn't that it might make you feel (momentarily) happy, but rather *it would be a very good thing to do.* Can we agree with that? Shall we take this verse as an endorsement of any vengeful action that *we* might wish to take?

Most people would say no, and they would be right. They would say, "No matter what the Bible says, this is not a good thing to do." Would we condemn them for abandoning the Bible, for denying the Word of God, if they said so? Hardly. But why not? Why wouldn't we condemn them—or ourselves—in the same situation? The verse is in the Bible, isn't it? Aren't we supposed to take the Bible as our guide?

One traditional way of dealing with this verse, and others like it, is to turn it into a moral allegory, treating it as something aimed at increasing individual virtue. Here, for instance, is C. S. Lewis in *Reflections on the Psalms,* speaking about the "cursing psalms":

> I know things in the inner world which are like babies; the
> infantile beginnings of small indulgences, small resentments,
> which may one day become dipsomania [i.e., alcoholism] or
> settled hatred, but which woo and wheedle us with special
> pleadings and seem so tiny, so helpless that in resisting them
> we feel we are being cruel to animals. They begin
> whimpering to us "I don't ask much, but", or "I had at least
> hoped", or "you owe yourself *some* consideration". Against all
> such pretty infants (the dears have such winning ways) the
> advice of the Psalm is the best. Knock the little bastards' brains
> out. And "blessed" he who can, for it's easier said than done. *

This is fine as an example of moral exhortation, but as a way of answering the question, "How do we accept the Bible's

* C. S. Lewis, *Reflections on the Psalms* (New York: Harcourt, Brace & World, 1958), chapter 12.

authority in the case of a verse like this?" it is useless. It never confronts what the text is in fact saying. The psalm is talking about a specific situation, an actual historical event, and insisting that it was so horrendous, and the behavior of the Babylonians so awful, that it would be right and moral to grab up a Babylonian baby—who, of course, could have had nothing to do, as an individual, with any atrocities whatsoever—and slaughter it in the most grisly way possible. As a guide to how to deal with the text as it is, C. S. Lewis is here in exactly the same position as an ardent radical dismissing Paul's views on women: he simply ignores what is in the text in favor of his own moral point of view.

What then can we say about revenge after reading such a text? Let us adopt a different approach. Let us look at the situation of Israel as it was in the ancient world, and see if it will give us a clue as to how to read this verse, without either ignoring it or condoning it.

The story of the Bible is the story of a small land that is caught in a world of political powers and forces much bigger than it is. This small land, Israel or Judah or Palestine, must deal with empires all around it: Egyptians, Assyrians, Babylonians, Persians, Greeks, and Romans. Furthermore, it must manage its relationships with other small states, such as Syria; with neighboring groups, such as the Philistines, the Amorites, and the Edomites; and with its own fellow-tribes when the country itself divides in two. Within this context this small land enjoys only brief periods of independence and self-rule, alternating with much longer periods of domination by the ruling powers in various periods, and conflict with the smaller states near at hand. The domination is sometimes only indirect, merely requiring the payment of monetary tribute or taxes; but sometimes it is direct, and that means that the outside power imposes or appoints its own rulers, who then extract the tribute while keeping the population quiet. Sometimes this domination means invasion or destruction; almost always it means impoverishment, oppression, struggle, and the constant threat of arrest or death for any who complain or resist.

Looking at this story as we do—as C. S. Lewis does—from our own perspective, we tend to concentrate on the moral or spiritual aspects of it as they apply to our own lives. We see ourselves struggling against our own selfishness, or striving to achieve our own potential as God's creation. We apply the ideas of liberation in the Bible to our own liberation from the habits or tendencies that enslave us. This is not wrong—the Bible itself talks this way—but in many cases, the specific texts are not talking about an individual moral effort, but a group task that is political, becoming the community that God is calling them to be. If we can step outside our own perspective—our citizenship in a superpower, our economic status, our cultural biases—this story looks very different. If we see it from the point of view of a Guatemalan, or a Nicaraguan, or a Zimbabwean, or a Rwandan, or a Somali, or an Indonesian, or even a New Zealander or Canadian, we will see it in a very different way.

As citizens of a global superpower, our temptations tend to be those of arrogance and indifference, of callous disregard for others. We can, with little effort, go for days or weeks without thinking about any other country on earth. Or, if we do think about them, it is usually in the context of our own empire: our need for raw materials, protecting our border from illegal entrants, the armies fighting our battles on the other side of the world. For the inhabitants of many of those smaller countries, however, such disregard of us would be an unimaginable luxury. It is not just that we may impinge upon them militarily; they are daily bombarded with our cultural exports, mostly movies and television shows. Their economies are often directly dependent on decisions made in our country; their leaders have to deal with us every day. We are inescapable.

For those in this situation—that of being citizens of a small and weak country—the temptations are those of subservience and resentment. When we look at the final verses of Psalm 137 in that light, therefore, we can read them in a somewhat different way. Those verses represent how a powerless group feels in a situation of oppression. "We'll remember the way our so-called 'friends' turned on us and joined the enemy side, seeing what they could get out of it! And the enemy—! May someone, someday, do to them what they did to us! May they suffer the way we suffered—the way they would suffer if someone killed their children in front of their eyes!"

Such a way of reading the end of the psalm does not make it "right," but it makes it understandable. It shows us what happens when people are treated unjustly, oppressed, exploited, or regarded with contempt. C. S. Lewis has noticed this, too, though he still keeps it on the level of individual morality and misses the central point of group responsibility when he writes that "the natural result of cheating a man, or 'keeping him down' or neglecting him, is to arouse resentment. . . . Such hatreds are the kind of thing that cruelty and injustice, by a sort of natural law, produce. This, among other things, is what wrongdoing means. Take from a man his freedom or his goods and you may have taken his innocence, almost his humanity, as well." * Lewis makes his point, but he does not go far enough and ignores the psalm's communal message. We can take from the biblical passage a clear moral, though not the moral that the author was concerned to put into it. The author wanted divine or, at least, human vengeance on the Babylonians, and thought that such vengeance was perfectly justifiable no matter how horrible a form it took.

For us, however, the moral message is somewhat different: "Look at the Babylonians, and see how the history of the oppressed peoples of their time has treated them. Think about how our country, in the present world situation, is behaving, and how it might appear from the point of view of someone who is on the bottom, rather than the top, of the international order. Surely, we do not want to be like the Babylonians!"

Outside of the mind of God, only history will tell whether we succeed or fail in that.

Visions of Judgment

In the New Testament, few passages, perhaps, are as difficult to read in the spirit in which they seem to have been written as the scenes of judgment in the Book of Revelation. The fall of "Babylon" (the book's code word for Rome) is part of a larger

* *Reflections on the Psalms*, chapter 3.

vision of destruction that avenges the persecution of the early
Christians. The entire vision of judgment occurs in chapters 18
through 20; we will look at excerpts to see what can be made of
them.

The destruction of the "great whore," Babylon, the kingdom
of all those opposed to God's rule, is narrated in chapter 18. Then
comes the reaction of those in heaven:

> After this I heard what seemed to be the loud voice of a great
> multitude in heaven, saying,
> "Hallelujah!
> Salvation and glory and power to our God,
> for his judgments are true and just;
> he has judged the great whore
> who corrupted the earth with her fornication,
> and he has avenged on her the blood of his servants."
> Once more they said,
> "Hallelujah!
> The smoke goes up from her forever and ever." (19.1–3)

This is followed by the vision of the victory of Christ:

> Then I saw heaven opened, and there was a white horse! Its
> rider is called Faithful and True, and in righteousness he
> judges and makes war. His eyes are like a flame of fire, and on
> his head are many diadems; and he has a name inscribed that
> no one knows but himself. He is clothed in a robe dipped in
> blood, and his name is called The Word of God. And the
> armies of heaven, wearing fine linen, white and pure, were
> following him on white horses. From his mouth comes a
> sharp sword with which to strike down the nations, and he
> will rule them with a rod of iron; he will tread the wine press
> of the fury of the wrath of God the Almighty. On his robe
> and on his thigh he has a name inscribed, "King of kings and
> Lord of lords."
> Then I saw an angel standing in the sun, and with a loud
> voice he called to all the birds that fly in midheaven, "Come,
> gather for the great supper of God, to eat the flesh of kings,

the flesh of captains, the flesh of the mighty, the flesh of horses and their riders—flesh of all, both free and slave, both small and great." Then I saw the beast and the kings of the earth with their armies gathered to make war against the rider on the horse and against his army. And the beast was captured, and with it the false prophet who had performed in its presence the signs by which he deceived those who had received the mark of the beast and those who worshiped its image. These two were thrown alive into the lake of fire that burns with sulfur. And the rest were killed by the sword of the rider on the horse, the sword that came from his mouth; and all the birds were gorged with their flesh. (19.11–21)

What are we to do with this incredible vision of universal slaughter at the hands of Christ, followed by the gorging of carrion birds on the corpses of the slain? How can we come away from this vision exhorting ourselves and each other to love our enemies and pray for our persecutors? Even though the vision is of *Christ*'s vengeance, not ours, the author of the passage seems to be exulting in the overthrow of those who are enemies of God.

The key, I believe, to all such passages in the Book of Revelation is to see them as symbolizing moral or spiritual combat, not literal combat. The sword with which the triumphant Christ slays his enemies is a *word,* not a literal sword: it comes forth from his mouth, and (since he is named Faithful, True, and The Word of God) it is the ultimate expression of God's truth and reliability, the full expression of who and what God is. The slaughter is, among other things, the death of falsehood in the presence of undeniable truth, and the death of betrayal when it is faced with utter reliability.

The vision is of a time when dissembling is no longer possible: the truth about God and Christ, the truth about morality, and the truth about God's love can no longer be denied. The beast and the whore, images of idolatry and the domination of life by wealth and power built upon military tyranny are flung into the burning lake because such misuse of power must be destroyed. The smoke of their burning goes up forever because the kingdom of God is one where power is subordinated to love, and therefore power exercised in oppression will perpetually be prevented.

Finally, the gorging of carrion birds on the flesh of the slaughtered foe is a grim and visceral image of the fact that, until truth is undeniable, falsehood and misrepresentation—fraud, spiritual lies, and immorality parading as morality—grow fat on the lives of those they mislead. When the truth is revealed, so is the true nature of all falsehood: it is carrion, death masquerading as life, only good to be fed to vultures. The growth of lies and fraud, during the time when truth is not so easy to discern, may seem like life—but in fact it is death.

A briefer example from the Psalms will extend the point. In Psalm 58, the psalmist prays for just retribution against "the wicked," who "err from their birth, speaking lies" (v. 3). As punishment, he asks God to "break the teeth in their mouths" (v. 6) —in other words, as they have used their mouths for falsehood, take the weapon away from them. But then, at the end, the psalmist says:

> The righteous will rejoice when they see vengeance done;
>   they will bathe their feet in the blood of the wicked.
> People will say, "Surely there is a reward for the righteous;
>   surely there is a God who judges on earth." (vv. 10–11)

Grisly though the image is, it may have conveyed more nuance to the original audience than it does to us. In the ancient world it was important for the recompense of the wicked to be publicly visible—to the righteous as well as everyone else—so that others can see that justice is being done. In addition, bathing one's feet, or having them washed, indicated superiority (see John 13.1–16). So with this imagery the "blood" (or, in biblical terms, the life) of the wicked is being subordinated to the righteous, so that a righteous life takes its proper place and the wicked are compelled to serve it. It is the duty of human beings to serve righteousness; this particular symbolic expression of that truth makes it very plain.

We seem, nevertheless, to have come a long way from Jesus'
exhortation to bless those who curse us and to pray for our enemies. In an even more extreme formulation, immediately pre-
ceding his command to love our enemies, Jesus has this to say:

> You have heard that it was said, "An eye for an eye and a tooth
> for a tooth" [Exodus 21.24]. But I say to you, Do not resist an
> evildoer. But if anyone strikes you on the right cheek, turn the
> other also; and if anyone wants to sue you and take your coat,
> give your cloak as well; and if anyone forces you to go one
> mile, go also the second mile. (Matthew 5.38–41)

Taken literally, and applied across the board, this exhortation
would make it impossible to work against injustice in any context. What can we do about it?

Look first at an Old Testament passage that, in effect, makes
some of the same points and may stand behind some of the for-
mulations in Jesus' statement:

> I offered my back to the floggers,
> And my cheeks to those who tore out my hair.
> I did not hide my face
> From insult and spittle. (Isaish 50.6, Tanakh)

> He was despised, shunned by men,
> A man of suffering, familiar with disease.
> As one who hid his face from us,
> He was despised, we held him of no account.
> Yet it was our sickness that he was bearing,
> Our suffering that he endured.
> We accounted him plagued,
> Smitten and afflicted by God;
> But he was wounded for our sins,
> Crushed because of our iniquities.
> He bore the chastisement that made us whole,
> And by his bruises we were healed.
> We all went astray like sheep,
> Each going his own way;
> And the LORD visited upon him

The guilt of all of us.
He was maltreated, yet he was submissive,
He did not open his mouth;
Like a sheep being led to the slaughter,
Like a ewe, dumb before those who shear her,
He did not open his mouth. (Isaiah 53.3–7, Tanakh)

We can see here that Jesus' exhortations to "turn the other cheek" and in other ways not to resist evil done to oneself echo, if they are not in fact directly inspired by, the prophet Isaiah's evocation of the Suffering Servant. We should not be surprised to see Jesus turning to the Hebrew Bible for this image of suffering love. The conventional, and mistaken, contrast between the Old Testament "God of wrath" and the New Testament "God of love" cannot last when one has read the Old Testament with attention. In addition, to speak of Jesus being inspired by his own Holy Scriptures—the Bible of Israel—is simply to acknowledge his human nature. He, like us, received truth from his surrounding culture, and that culture included "the *torah* of Moses, the prophets, and the psalms" (Luke 24.44), the traditional threefold division of the Bible according to Jewish use.

Still, what are we to make of these exhortations that we should accept evil done to us, and be passive in the face of mistreatment? I think we can look at the Isaiah passage in the following way, and then use it as a clue for understanding Jesus' exhortation from the Sermon on the Mount.

First, look at the statements in the passage that the (unnamed) servant "was wounded for our sins, crushed because of our iniquities." Simply on the basic level of life in society, we see examples of this all around us. To take an obvious one: wealthy, first-world consumers, by their purchases and lifestyles, cause pollution greater than that caused by poor people. Much of the polluting activity, however—factory runoff, power plants with insufficient filtering, and so on—takes place elsewhere, and much of it is sited in poverty-stricken areas, either poor communities in the United States or poor countries elsewhere in the world. The inhabitants of these communities thus suffer from diseases—

cancer, birth defects, increased asthma rates—that are brought about by pollution that has its ultimate cause elsewhere. It is the simple truth to say of an individual resident of one of these places, "It was our sickness that he was bearing, our suffering that he endured."

And what of the matter of being submissive, of not resisting evil done to oneself? It is necessary to move very carefully here, especially for those who are in positions of power relative to most of the rest of the world. It is very easy to take such passages and make them the rationale for suppressing efforts on the part of the poor and oppressed to obtain justice. Exhortations to passivity, when the one doing the exhorting will benefit from the passivity of the one being exhorted, are always suspect. But there is a different sense in which not reacting when evil is done to oneself can actually be a transformative act, a way of breaking an endless cycle of violence or wrongdoing.

Look at our world, and all of the evil perpetrated in it. Much of this evil is done in order to gain an advantage, or to seize something of value: natural resources, access to markets, and so on. But there is a good deal of evil that is committed entirely or mostly in response to other evil. Just as those who are abused—psychologically, physically, sexually—can grow up to become abusers themselves, so, as W. H. Auden put it in his poem on the outbreak of war, "September 1, 1939":

> I and the public know
> What all schoolchildren learn,
> Those to whom evil is done
> Do evil in return.

Those to whom evil is done even commit evil acts against those who had nothing to do with the original evil. They bash the heads of the babies of their enemies. They undertake terror attacks, not to avenge themselves against those who have attacked them, but to force others, whom they see as indifferent, to feel their pain as they themselves feel it. They engage—we engage—in reprisals against civilian populations for the crimes of their leaders, or in wars against others in reaction to attacks on ourselves by someone else. Others seemingly can never put behind them wrongs done not directly to themselves, but to their ancestors, and must continue to fight, not against those who perpetrated those long-ago wrongs, but against their descendants. And those descendants themselves fight back.

Such is the character of large parts of our world. Looked at from the outside, it would seem to be the very definition of insanity: perpetual cycles of violence and wrongdoing, with no obvious exit. That is why the seemingly insane act of not resisting evil done to oneself can in fact be the sanest response of all. It can be the nakedly honest statement of anyone who says, "Here is where it stops. I am no longer going to continue this repetition of retaliation. I am going to create the world anew by not responding in kind." The beaten child who will not himself grow up to become an abuser; the oppressed person who will not kill her oppressor; the victims of apartheid who drew back from avenging themselves on their former masters—these are the ones who exemplify what it means to act according to Jesus' words. And they have lived out Paul's exhortation as well: "Do not be overcome by evil, but overcome evil with good."

Paul certainly "misread" Deuteronomy. But he did so in obedience to a far deeper meaning in the Old Testament, one that was emphasized also in Jesus' teaching. Deuteronomy warned the Israelites—and presumably us as well—that the consequences of our own bad actions could very well come back to cause us grief, at a later date. In our current context, we can think of global warming in this way: our energy profligacy may end up causing us increased drought or flooding, violent storms and erosion of coastlines, and so on. Paul, and Jesus, responding to evil in a different context and bringing forward a different part of the Old Testament, warn us that the real and steep path out of vengeance may require of us one of the greatest sacrifices we can make, short of giving up our lives altogether: the sacrifice of refusing to act on our own urge to retaliate against those who have hurt us. The Dirty Harry who lives within each of us will have to die. He can be reborn—but only in his character of an advocate of justice for the powerless and a foe of oppression, not in that of his angry vengefulness. In God's good time, the only way to "make my day" is to follow the narrower, steeper way: "Do not be overcome by evil, but overcome evil with good." "By his bruises we were healed."

LOVING OUR ENEMIES

Does the Bible Coddle Villains?

IN 1994, A MINISTER of the Church of Christ in Madison, Wisconsin, baptized "Jeff," a young man in prison.* Jeff had asked to be baptized, and Pastor Roy Ratcliff had been contacted by the prison authorities and had agreed to do it. They met and discussed Christian faith for a few weeks, and then Pastor Ratcliff baptized Jeff and welcomed him to God's family.

"Jeff" was Jeffrey Dahmer, the serial killer who had murdered seventeen young men and boys. (A few months after his baptism, Dahmer was himself murdered in prison.)

The article by Dan Barry, "He Befriended a Serial Killer, and Opened the Door to God," also relates the response of others to Pastor Ratcliff's acceptance of Jeffrey Dahmer into the Christian community.

> People would walk away when introduced to him or argue that they wanted no part of a heaven that included Jeffrey Dahmer. Some would praise him to his face, only to tell others that he had been duped. He was rarely invited to other churches to talk about the salvation of the least of us, because, he guesses, "there is a sense of shame."
>
> At gatherings of preachers in the region, he says, one minister from Milwaukee constantly points him out to others

* *New York Times,* Sunday, March 11, 2007, A20.

and says: Do you know who that man is? Do you know what he did?

Such a deed, and our reactions (as well as the reactions of others) to it, can throw into stark relief our real beliefs about the universality of God's call and how far the love of God can reach. It can also bring us to reflect on how we ourselves put into practice some of the biblical exhortations that, presumably, we believe we are supposed to be carrying out. These commands are sometimes not as prominent in our thinking as the biblical prohibitions, but they can cause us trouble nonetheless.

By his actions, Pastor Roy Ratcliff was carrying out the command to baptize in the name of the Father, Son, and Holy Spirit. The Bible contains many other positive commands. By "positive commands" I mean those that exhort to a specific action, rather than those that prohibit us from doing something. The grammatical form of the command—"Do this, do not do that"—is not what is of primary importance. A command to "refrain from" something or other—stealing, lying, envying—is positive grammatically, but negative in action; a command that we should "never cease to" do something or other—speak the truth, worship God—is negative grammatically but positive in action.

Among the commandments in the Sermon on the Mount, Jesus includes the following:

> You have heard that it was said, "You shall love your neighbor
> and hate your enemy." But I say to you, Love your enemies
> and pray for those who persecute you, so that you may be
> children of your Father in heaven; for he makes his sun rise
> on the evil and on the good, and sends rain on the righteous
> and on the unrighteous. For if you love those who love you,
> what reward do you have? Do not even the tax collectors do
> the same? And if you greet only your brothers and sisters,
> what more are you doing than others? Do not even the
> Gentiles do the same? Be perfect, therefore, as your heavenly
> Father is perfect. (Matthew 5.43–48)

We have to get one or two matters out of the way before we can look at this passage more closely. First, unlike some other passages in the Sermon on the Mount, Jesus' words here—"You have heard," followed by a saying—are not a quotation from the Hebrew Bible. There is a statement in Leviticus 19.18 about loving one's neighbor but there is no command from God, or any statement anywhere, that one should hate one's enemies. In other words, the idea that Jesus is criticizing here is one that describes a natural human behavior, not one that arises from the moral tradition of Judaism or of the Hebrew Bible.

How shall we describe that natural human behavior? In its essence, it is our behavior when we expect to be treated in ways that are appropriate to how *we* behave, so that when we invite someone to dinner, they invite us in return, rewarding favor for favor. Jesus is not so much condemning this behavior as he is pointing out its moral emptiness. Most of us begin our emotional lives by "loving" where we have been loved, or where we expect love in return—we begin by loving our caregivers. And, later in life (if we are lucky, much later), we encounter those who do us harm, either carelessly or deliberately, and we "hate" those people. We have, in other words, returned love for goodness and hate for harm. But, Jesus says, this is not how God loves.

Because this exhortation ends with the words "Be perfect," it has sometimes been called a "counsel of perfection," an ideal that is held before us to show us what life in the kingdom of God would be like, but which is not meant to be applied literally in our life-circumstances now. I am not sure, however, that we can solve the difficulties of this passage in such a way. For one thing, the command is certainly set in the context of the present: "Your enemies" are equated with "those who persecute you." Then, too, the example of God's perfection that is given—"he makes his sun rise on the evil and on the good, and sends rain on the righteous and on the unrighteous"—describes what God is doing *now*, not in some idealized future. The whole tendency of the exhortation is toward action in the present, not toward the contemplation of a future perfection.

When people reflect on such a passage, they sometimes make it harder on themselves by imagining trying to love someone—someone close to them or someone well-known to them—who has done them great harm. A brutalizing parent, an unfaithful lover, a cheating business partner—such are the people who might spring to mind when we think about "our enemies." Or, perhaps, our enemies are not intimate enemies but instead strangers who have directly harmed us or those we love—thieves, alcoholic homicidal drivers, rapists, murderers. While clearly Jesus' words would apply to such cases, it is probably not wise to start at such an exalted level. We must crawl before we can walk. Let us go back to a lower point and try an example by which we may be able to work our way forward.

Think about your reactions to other drivers when you are on the road in your car. How do you feel when someone cuts you off?—or beats you out of the light?—or cuts ahead of you in line?—or passes you on the wrong side? Do you reflect objectively on their transgression of the rules of the road—assuming that they have actually transgressed—or do you fume as if they had insulted you to your face? In the experience of most people I know, such driving infractions on the part of others can be infuriating, regardless of whether they represent any actual danger, precisely because the offender seems to have targeted you but, insulated in his or her little bubble of glass and steel, sails blithely on, unconcerned with you and disregarding how you have been treated.

Suppose we regard those other drivers as "our enemies." What happens when we try to pray for them? If I can trust my own experience, this is a difficult thing to do. When I try to determine why this is so difficult, even later after any anger I might have felt at the behavior has subsided, I am usually driven back to the same point. I have to get past the idea, nonsensical though it might be, that the offending driver acted deliberately in order to irritate me. In other words, I must not "take it personally."

Reflecting on such examples of bad driving can bring several issues to the foreground. First, the essential step in praying for "my enemies" is to get myself out of the way—not in the sense of ignoring what has happened that has concerned me, since that is the occasion of my prayer, but in the sense of disregarding or downplaying the fact that it has happened *to me*. That is, I must stop taking offense at the supposed insult and try to look at it objectively, as if it had happened to someone else.

A second issue follows from this. In looking at the facts as objectively as I can, I need to acknowledge that the person who engaged in the behavior that annoyed me was not doing so with the specific view of annoying me. He was driving as he did for his own purposes, not in order to have an effect upon me. He *did* have an effect upon me, and that is the occasion for my prayer, but he was driving as he did for some other purpose—because he was in a hurry, because he was thinking about something else, even, perhaps, because he was habitually a bad driver. It was just my (bad) luck that I was in his path that day.

The third issue, therefore, is the need for me to separate the quality of *the action as it is without reference to me in particular* from *the action as it has an impact on me*. In other words, I can still condemn the action itself—the person's actions may be rude, or inconsiderate, or reckless—but separate it from my feelings of offense that it impinged upon me.

Finally, I also need to separate the action from the doer. In those cases where a stranger has done something I find annoying, my temptation is to characterize the person by the action. "What a rude, inconsiderate slob!" I think to myself. But that is more than I know. I may have witnessed an inconsiderate action, but I don't know that it was performed by an inconsiderate person. It may have been uncharacteristic. Maybe she was having a bad day. Maybe he just heard some upsetting news. Would *I* want to be judged by the character of the worst of my actions? Would I even want to be judged on the basis of a random selection of my actions on a given day?

Praying for Our Enemies
We may seem to have gone far afield from Jesus' command, but all of these reflections and the issues we have uncovered will come into play in our next effort to see how Jesus' words might

apply in our contemporary lives. To do so, we will engage in a little "thought experiment."

Think back to 1990, when our government was preparing to battle the Iraqi armed forces in Kuwait, and to early 1991, when that war actually took place. Think back also to 2002, when our government was preparing to invade Iraq, and to the years following the invasion of March 19, 2003: the defeat of the Iraqi armed forces, the conquest of Baghdad, and the aftermath of the invasion and occupation.

Now, imagine the following. Suppose that there had been an organized effort, in 1990 and again in 2002, among the leaders of all of the U.S. Christian churches, to put Jesus' command into effect. Suppose that these leaders had gotten together, all of them—Methodists, Presbyterians, Baptists, Episcopalians, Roman Catholics, Eastern Orthodox, Pentecostal, Free Church, Congregationalists, Lutherans, Unitarians; all of the leadership structure of the National Council of Churches, of the National Association of Evangelicals, the Orthodox Churches in America, the U.S. Conference of Catholic Bishops—and issued the following proclamation:

> We, the leaders of the Christian churches in the United States
> of America, despite what other issues may still divide us, wish
> to unite in applying Jesus' words to the current international
> crisis with regard to the coming conflict between America
> and the nation of Iraq. We call on all Christians to meditate
> on the words of Our Lord and Savior Jesus Christ, "Love your
> enemies and pray for those who persecute you" (Matthew
> 5.44). We further urge every Christian pastor to lead his or
> her congregation, on every Sunday from now until our
> hostilities with Iraq have ceased, in prayer for the Iraqi leader,
> Saddam Hussein, and for the people of Iraq.

What might have been the result of such an appeal? Would anyone have carried it out? Would pastors and congregations in fact have prayed for Saddam?

Perhaps they would have. Perhaps such prayers would have resulted, if not in peace, at least in the recognition, on the part of those Christians undertaking them, of the humanity we share with Saddam and with the Iraqi people. (I do not mean to imply anything about non-Christians in saying this. Non-Christians, and indeed nonreligious people, are completely capable of seeing the humanity of their fellow human beings. The point of this mental exercise is to imagine what might have happened if Christians had put into effect a specific, direct command of the person they claim to revere above all others.) Perhaps, given this recognition of our shared humanity, such abuses against individual Iraqis as those at Abu Ghraib would not have taken place. Perhaps when Saddam Hussein was captured there would have been no gloating.

Perhaps. But honesty compels me to say, it is far more likely that there would have been a nationwide outcry at such a proposal. Denunciations would have poured in—from Congress, from newspaper editorials and columnists, from talk radio hosts, from the web—questioning the patriotism, even the sanity, of those issuing the proclamation. If any pastors tried to implement it, members of congregations would have stormed out of church, or stood and angrily denounced their leaders. Campaigns would have sprung up to withhold contributions from any church or denomination that dared to pray for Saddam Hussein.

Which is more likely, in your view?

Now think about what might lie behind such a negative reaction. Note the similarities between what springs to mind about praying for Saddam Hussein and praying for someone who has impinged on us and annoyed us personally.

First, praying for Saddam would have forced us to think about how much of our hostility to him was ego-driven. What part of the lead-up to the Persian Gulf and Iraq wars was involved, not with any actual threat, but with our sense of national honor? In the case of the invasion of Iraq, we were also still dealing with the aftermath of the terror attacks of September 11, 2001. Could we have reflected usefully on whether that was influencing our need to go to war?

Second, it would have helped bring to the fore consideration of what Saddam was actually up to. As we now know, after the

invasion, the purported reason for it—Saddam's supposed possession of chemical, biological, and nuclear weapons, and the
threat that he might use them against us or provide them to others to use against us—was wrong. Had a significant part of the
U.S. population been praying for Saddam, we might have had
more patience in trying to find out the truth about what indeed
his capabilities were, and how much of a threat he actually was.

Third, we could have looked at what Saddam was doing, or
purportedly doing, as it was in itself. We could have tried to put
ourselves in his place, to understand why someone with a dangerous, larger neighbor, such as Iran, might want to give the
impression that he was dangerous, too. We might also understand—without condoning—why Iraq, with its volatile mix of
groups with long-simmering, historical hatred for one another
who had been yoked together by violence more than eighty
years ago, might have ended up with a ruler who was a brutal
dictator.

Finally, we could have reflected usefully on what it was necessary to do, and how it was necessary to do it, if we decided to
rid Iraq of Saddam Hussein, because we could reflect on Saddam's actions and not on the person of Saddam himself. Thus, the
invasion would become not "toppling Saddam" but "reestablish-
ing Iraq" and our assessment of military strength might have
needed adjustment. By all accounts, Saddam was a brutal, even
pathological figure. But national policy cannot be tied solely, or
even primarily, to our sense of the moral worth of the leaders of
other countries. If it were, we would be perpetually at war, or at
least in perpetual contention with numerous leaders around the
globe. Had we been praying for the welfare of the Iraqi people,
we would perhaps have been more willing to look at what was
really needed to better their circumstances: much more of a
commitment to control postwar chaos (chaos that was exten-
sively predicted beforehand); much more of a worldwide, or at
least region-wide, effort; and much more of a financial commitment to rebuilding, even at the cost of some financial sacrifice on
our part.

I do not wish to be misunderstood. The judgment about whether to go to war, in either of these circumstances, is not at issue. The issue is, assuming that we are a nation the majority of whose population is Christian, should we have been praying for Saddam Hussein and the Iraqis? And, if we had, would it have made a difference in how we went to war? Should we have tried to put into practice a precept that Jesus Christ gave to us as a direct command? And do we believe that if we had followed the command of Jesus in this regard, it would have made a difference to our behavior later on? Do we, in fact, take the words of Jesus with utmost seriousness?

There is one aspect of loving our enemies and praying for those who persecute us that we have not touched on, but that would affect how we would love or pray and how we would think about loving or praying. It will be clearer if once again I use a personal example. If I pray for an alcoholic acquaintance, as I have done in the past, I am not praying that she be granted a new liver so as to be enabled to go on drinking to excess. I am praying for her liberation from a burden of addiction. In other words, I am praying for her good, not for support in continuing on a destructive course. Praying for Saddam Hussein would be the same kind of thing: not "Help him in his brutal dictatorial ways" but "Help him to see that he can be other and better than he is" or at least "Help to stop him from continuing to do wrong, for his own sake as well as for the sake of others."

True Benevolence

We have not, however, dealt with the final and most difficult part of Jesus' exhortation. That is the part about how we should imitate our heavenly Father, who sends sunshine and rain—in other words, all the necessities of life for an agricultural society—to the just and the unjust. What would it mean to "be like" God in this respect? And how would it qualify us to "be perfect"?

Taken literally, of course, this command makes no sense. We cannot make the sun shine or the rain fall, in any way that matters. Areas of the earth still suffer drought and flood and all kinds of weather-related catastrophes, and, although we can mitigate the consequences, we cannot prevent the occurrence. So we must think about how we can "be like" God in ways appropriate to our actual situation.

We should note first that, whatever else that remark is, it is an accurate description of things as they are. The blessings of life— health, fortunate circumstances, good luck in business, talents and abilities—are distributed among the members of the human race without any regard, seemingly, for moral worth. Rain or drought happen to farmers no matter whether they are good or bad persons. Musical talent, poetical creativity, artistic ability, a beautiful singing voice—all are granted to people of vastly differing moral character. Even physical beauty, as we all learn to our dismay as we go through life, is not correlated with morality in any way. The rain and the sunshine do indeed come alike to the righteous and the unrighteous.

But we must also note what the exhortation is guarding against. We must not attempt ourselves to adjust the rewards of life according to moral deserts. In this way, Jesus' exhortation is not so much a "counsel of perfection" as it is a "counsel of imperfection." We simply do not know enough to make the judgments that would be required to bring goodness and good fortune into alignment. And Jesus is telling us that God does not do that either, whatever God may choose to do in the future. So we should not take into account our own view of someone's moral worth (or lack of it) in determining how we will behave toward them. We should behave as we would behave regardless of who would be helped or hurt by our actions. We ought to do the right thing even when someone we disapprove of will benefit, or someone we love would be harmed. And, conversely, even if someone we love would benefit, we cannot do something wrong—nor can we commit a wrong in order to harm an enemy.

More than this, however, is implied. As Jesus goes on to note, everyone acts so as to benefit those we love, or to benefit someone who can repay us with a good deed. This is normal human behavior, not very exalted in a moral sense. The real test of benevolence, therefore, comes when we are called to extend it

either to someone who has no intention of reciprocating it—
one's "enemy"—or to someone who is incapable of returning
the favor: a poor person, the inhabitant of a far-away country,
someone who is sick or dying, someone who is in prison. That
is what it means to "be like" God.

What I think we may take away from the exhortation is this:
so far as in us lies, we must come to treat all human beings as
even-handedly as we can. It is not for us to adjust the moral cal-
culus of the universe. If we owe someone something, that someone should receive it from us, whether we like the person or
not—and whether the person has acted well by us in the past or
not. In the case of Saddam Hussein, we owed him at least a fair
assessment of what he was up to and what threat he posed to us.
He should not have been a convenient victim whom we could
topple simply to show how strong we were. He had had nothing to do with attacking us on September 11, 2001; whatever
his intentions for the future—intentions that we could speculate
about, but not know for sure—our actions should have been
predicated on what he had done, not what we (on perhaps flimsy
grounds) feared he might do.

Putting this command into practice could well be the most
difficult thing we could ever do as Christians. It would certainly
subject us to withering criticism from other Americans—including other Christians. We can certainly come to identify with Pastor Roy Ratcliff, the man who baptized Jeffrey Dahmer, and his
experiences of being ostracized even within the Christian community in which he is a leader. The cost of following Jesus' command can mean social isolation, the condemnation of those who
know us, and, if we are prominent enough (a politician, a
celebrity), even mockery and denunciations from radio talk show
hosts and television commentators. All this for praying for Saddam Hussein.

Should that surprise us?

JUSTICE

Is What We Need What We Deserve?

AN OLD COMEDY routine depicts the organizational meeting of the Society of Anarchists. The person convening the meeting is shown saying, "Very well then—it's agreed. There will be no rules." From the floor, someone shouts out, "I think there have to be *some* rules!" But the convener stands firm: "Sorry— those are the rules."

It is virtually impossible to maintain a group in cohesive fashion without some rules. Like the groups themselves, these rules are of various sorts. Some may be called rules of social interaction—not blocking the aisles of a grocery store, for instance. It is not illegal to block the aisles, but if you do you will be subjected to a constant stream of "Excuse me!" "Pardon me!" and less polite comments from those around you. Other rules govern behavior in specific contexts—concert halls, houses of worship, courts of law. Games have rules, for both players and bystanders.

Other rules are more formal so that people who have no acquaintance with each other can interact effectively. Buying and selling are governed by rules. There are traffic rules, workplace rules, classroom rules. And there are laws, lots of them. For the most part laws serve a larger purpose: making human interactions fairer, safer, more reliable, however we want to express it. We have laws limiting behavior, laws mandating behavior, laws governing who may do certain things, laws refereeing between people engaged in a joint activity. And we change laws all the time, in response to new conditions or given evidence of the failure of current laws to do what we had intended them to do. We clearly have an idea of something behind our rules and laws, which they are trying to bring about and against which they can be judged. We can regard laws as ineffective, as unfair, as biased. All of these things mean that the laws relate to some other thing. Our usual name for that thing is justice.

Although the Bible has a good deal to say about justice, unfortunately it does not present the topic in an organized way. Instead, we find a jumble of specific rules and regulations governing various situations; various broad statements (some in the Pentateuch, some in the prophets, some in the gospels, some in the New Testament letters) that may or may not apply in general circumstances; historical accounts in which characters may or may not be punished according to their deserts; and proposals for ideal communities in which justice is the organizing principle. From this mass of materials it is possible to draw different conclusions, depending on which parts of it one wants to emphasize; which principles one regards as providing the main foundation for explication; which parts one regards as applicable to current situations; and which parts one sees as idealizations or predictions of what will occur in an eschatological future.

In trying to understand these various strands, it may be best to begin by looking at the way some words for justice and related concepts are used in the Bible.

In the Hebrew Bible, "justice" (*mishpat* and related forms of the word) has a wider field of reference than the English word. The verb from which the noun is derived, *shaphat,* means primarily "render judgment, govern, apply the law"; but it also means "distinguish between good and bad." Thus, Psalm 82 says:

> God stands in the divine assembly;
>> among the divine beings He pronounces
>>> judgment [*yishpat*].
> How long will you judge [*tishpatu*] perversely,
>> showing favor to the wicked?

> Judge [*shiphtu*] the wretched and the orphan,
>   vindicate [*hatsdiqu*] the lowly and the poor.
>   (Psalm 82.1–3, Tanakh)

Here the same word, in different forms, appears and shifts from meaning "gives the final decision" to "decides wrongly" to "come in on the side of." God, in the performance of justice, condemns the "divine beings" to death for their unjust justice (v. 7), and proclaims the need for just judgment on behalf of those who are needy and oppressed. This meaning of intervention on behalf of the oppressed is clear in the use of the word *shophetim* for the title of the book that comes after the Book of Joshua in the Hebrew Bible (called the Book of Judges in our English versions), and for the use of the word in various forms to describe the various persons in the book and their actions. Othniel is said to become a *shophet* (3.10); Deborah *shophtah* Israel. To translate the word in all these places as "judge," though that is what traditional Bible versions do, is misleading. "Vindicator" or "champion" or "rescuer" would be much closer to the meaning given the way the words are used.

In the parallel structure of Psalm 82.3, where "judge" and "vindicate" appear as partial synonyms (linked with "the wretched and the orphan" and "the lowly and the poor," respectively), we have a link between terms that also appears in other passages—the word for "justice" and that for "righteousness" (*tsedeq* and various other forms). "Righteousness" is both the goal and the ground of justice. Consider two other passages where these terms are closely linked.

The first is in Isaiah's vision of the vineyard (Israel) and the beloved (God) (5.1–10). Near the end of the vision in which the vineyard has not produced the grapes that the beloved had expected, the prophet declares:

> . . . he expected justice [*mishpat*],
>   but saw bloodshed [*mispach*];
> righteousness [*tsedaqah*],
>   but heard a cry [*tse'aqah*]! (5.7)

The Hebrew puns in this prophetic statement, clearly equating "bloodshed" and "cry [of distress]," serve to emphasize the parallelism between the words for "justice" and "righteousness."

The second passage is from Amos 5.21–24, the climax of the prophet's great denunciation of empty worship. After repudiating festivals, sacrifices, and musical worship, God sets forth what is the result of true worship:

> . . . let justice [*mishpat*] roll down like waters,
>   and righteousness [*tsedaqah*] like an
>   ever-flowing stream. (5.24)

This meaning is also clear in Zechariah:

> Thus says the LORD of hosts: Render true judgments [*mishpat*], show kindness and mercy to one another; do not oppress the widow, the orphan, the alien, or the poor; and do not devise evil in your hearts against one another. (7.9–10)

"Justice," therefore, is more than merely making a decision according to the applicable laws; it is also a means of bringing about the true state of affairs that God wishes to be the case. That is why "righteousness" is so important in understanding what justice is supposed to be. The word (*tsedeq*) in essence means what is true, straight, right, or correct. Thus, according to Deuteronomy 25.13–15:

> You shall not have in your bag two kinds of weights, large and small. You shall not have in your house two kinds of measures, large and small. You shall have only a full and honest [*tsedeq*] weight; you shall have only a full and honest [*tsedeq*] measure.

The righteousness here applies not just to the honesty of the merchant, who is not supposed to buy by weight or volume using weights and measures that make the weight or the volume of what is being purchased seem smaller than it actually is (by using bigger measures), or to sell by weight or volume using weights and measures that make the weight or volume appear to be larger than it actually is (by using smaller measures). The righteousness, the trueness, is in the measures themselves. They are, or should be, according to what God wants.

When we turn to the New Testament, we see the same linkage between justice and righteousness, here made even easier by the fact that the same root lies behind the words for "justice" and "righteousness" in Greek. The root word *dike* (pronounced like "decay") originally meant "what was customary, right," in other words, "the right way of acting in a given situation," and its derivatives, *dikaios, dikaiosyne, dikaio,* and so on, mean "justice," "righteousness," or "to make just, righteous," that is, "to justify." They convey the idea that one's actions and indeed one's being are to be conformed to God's standard, and that God has taken steps to make this standard available to us in our thoughts and actions.

In one brief paragraph in the letter to the Romans, Paul presents this idea by means of repetitive use of the word in its various forms:

> But now, quite independently of law, though with the law and
> the prophets bearing witness to it, the righteousness
> [*dikaiosyne*] of God has been made known; it [i.e., this
> righteousness, *dikaiosyne*] is effective through faith in Christ
> for all who have such faith—all, without distinction. For all
> alike have sinned, and are deprived of the divine glory; and all
> are justified [*dikaioumenoi*] by God's free grace alone, through
> his act of liberation in the person of Christ Jesus. For God
> designed him to be the means of expiating sin by his death,
> effective through faith. God meant by this to demonstrate his
> justice [*dikaiosynes*], because in his forbearance he had
> overlooked the sins of the past—to demonstrate his justice
> now in the present, showing that he is himself just [*dikaion*]
> and also justifies [*dikaiounta*] anyone who puts his faith in
> Jesus. (Romans 3.21–26, Revised English Bible)

The source of justice and righteousness is God. God is the true standard toward which we must aim—to "fall short of the glory of God" does not mean to be human and not God-like, but rather to fall short of the true measure of what it means to be human. This is what Jesus himself is getting at in the Sermon on the Mount, when he calls for an ethic in which not merely action (adultery, murder) but inner inclination (lust, anger) are what we must resist and repent of. The issue is not that we must be ever harder on ourselves, but that we should be integral beings, whose outer expression is truly indicative of what is inside us. It is not enough if we do not act on our impulses of murderous rage; we need to get to the point where we do not harbor murderous thoughts at all. This is the reason, as well, that for Jesus the worst thing one can be is to be a hypocrite. Calling someone a hypocrite is the most devastating critique he can make of a person. To attend to one's outward demeanor *only,* disregarding the inner reality of one's personality and inclinations, is spiritually very dangerous. We are called to be "all of a piece": wholly just, wholly righteous, wholly conformed to the standards that express the truth of God. It is only on this basis that we can determine what is just and right in a given circumstance. We cannot apply a particular rule to make this determination; in effect, we are applying our very persons, as those persons have been redeemed and remade by God.

This lengthy discussion has been necessary because it is vital to understand the biblical conception of law, and the Bible's view of the relationship between law and justice. Like all law codes, biblical law has to be concerned with externalities: with the acts and behavior of people. It cannot regulate the inner life. Nonetheless, in both Old and New Testaments, the ultimate concern of justice is the rightness of the person: one's conformity to the absolute righteousness of God, as that can be expressed within any given human personality. This is knowable, of course, only to God (in a complete sense) and to the person himself or herself (always allowing for some self-delusion, since that seems inevitable). The outward behavior of a fully integrated human being, aligned to the righteousness of God, and that of a human being who acted not from moral impulse, but purely in order to avoid punishment or to gain some reward, could be indistinguishable to a third party. This is the inescapable dilemma on which all efforts to form moral commonwealths, theocracies, and utopian communities founder. We will look at one such current effort in examining the topic of criminal justice and law in the Bible.

The Bible's Criminal Code Revisited

Within the conservative Protestant movement in the United States, a small contingent of teachers and preachers has adopted the position that the only sound legal system, and therefore the one the United States should ultimately adopt if it wishes to be a moral nation, is the system set out in the Pentateuch: the biblical law code. This is not some casual proposal to recriminalize adultery. The proponents of this view believe that the entirety of the biblical criminal code should be our criminal code, including all of the penalties (stoning, severing of limbs, etc.) that are set out in the Bible and making illegal all of the actions that the Bible condemns.

This movement is known as "Christian Reconstructionism," and its theological position is called "Theocratic Dominionism."* This position was articulated by a conservative Presbyterian minister named R. J. Rushdoony in *Institutes of Biblical Law* and has been carried on by, among others, David Chilton, also a minister and Rushdoony's son-in-law. The proponents of this view maintain that, for example, adultery, homosexual relationships, and juvenile delinquency should be punishable by death, and that other crimes should be punished by mutilation, fines, and so forth, as is spelled out in the law codes of the Pentateuch.

Most people, when this view is presented to them, oppose it. Many find it horrifying. Nevertheless, the proponents of this view have one very significant argument in its favor, among those who believe that the Bible should be the ultimate rule of our moral life: none of these laws (unlike dietary restrictions or distinctive clothing, for instance) were repudiated by the early Christian church. The early Christians, of course, lived under the Roman legal system, and had no power to carry out the Bible's criminal justice system. (The Jews living at the time did not have such power, either. As the religious authorities point out to Pontius Pilate [John 18.31], they could not put anyone to death—

---

* It is described in an article in *Public Eye,* a policy magazine, and is available at www.publiceye.org/magazine/v08n1/chrisrec.html.

only the Romans could do that. So Jesus was not stoned to death, which would have been the Jewish penalty; he was crucified, a Roman punishment.) But according to the argument of these conservative Christians, when the church *is* in a position to establish the legal system in a particular geographic area, it should impose biblical law, since that law was handed down from God and therefore represents the only real blueprint for a righteous society. If we have the power to establish biblical law in the United States, we should do it so that America can truly be a godly, Christian commonwealth.

To evaluate this proposal, rather than looking at a wide range of biblical laws—do we really want to return to the days when wives were their husbands' property (Exodus 20.17) and daughters were their fathers' (Exodus 21.7)?—we can instead concentrate on the one that gives us the most trouble: the death penalty. In order to think about this reasonably, we have to try to view death not as we see it in our current, highly medicalized context: many people never actually see anyone die; death takes place behind a hospital or nursing home wall. In addition, death is now increasingly medicated for us, so that any suffering associated with it is greatly reduced or eliminated.

Death in biblical times, on the other hand—indeed, in all historical times up until the very recent past, in the developed world—was a prospect of discomfort and possibly of extreme pain for almost everyone. It was an unpleasant prospect for a number of reasons. For one thing, death came at a young age for a great many people. Those who did survive the diseases and dangers of infancy and childhood were regularly at risk for an early and uncomfortable death. Women often died in childbirth. Many people, when faced with failed crops, simply starved to death. Still others died of painful diseases and injuries, since medical care was rudimentary, there was nothing available to treat infections if the injury was an open wound, and there was no way to operate to stop internal bleeding. And, of course, people died as a result of violence—either directly, as in murder or wartime slaughter, or indirectly, as a result of being injured.

In many of these cases, death would not be quick. We need to bear in mind the general background of sickness, pain, and death in the ancient world, and indeed in the world well into the nineteenth century, when we look at the ways in which ancient societies carried out punishments in their criminal codes. In our world we have a reasonable belief that we will be able to escape most of the physical pain inherent in the human condition, but we forget that this is a relatively recent phenomenon. Most of the medical advances we now take for granted are barely a century old, and many of them were not available before the 1940s.

The imposition of the death penalty in ancient societies—indeed, in nearly all societies up until the eighteenth century or so in Europe—was a barbaric proceeding, to modern sensibilities. For one thing, it was imposed for a wide variety of offenses—not just for murder or other violent crime, but for theft, poaching of game, and blasphemy. For another, most executions were public events, conducted in areas where large crowds could gather and enjoy the proceedings. Finally, in many cases the method of execution was deliberately drawn-out and painful.

In the Bible, there are four methods of execution that are described or mandated. A few crimes were punishable by burning. People are put to death by the sword (stabbing or beheading). "Hanging"—actually a Persian method of execution better described as impalement—is referred to (for instance, in Esther 2.23 and 9.13). (Impalement was a particularly grisly method of execution, in which the victim was lowered over, and impaled upon, a sharpened stake that was planted in the ground. Death came slowly and with much pain.) Finally, the main method of execution in the Bible is death by stoning.

Although the procedure is not described, it is quite clear what would happen. The victim—whether secured, encircled, or pursued—would be pelted with stones until injured enough to die. This could mean a fractured skull; broken ribs leading to a punctured lung and suffocation; or fatal injury to internal organs. Such a death was, effectively, equivalent to being beaten to death. Fortunate victims were rendered unconscious early in the proceedings by a blow to the head. Unlucky ones could linger in a semiconscious state, presumed dead but unable to move because of broken bones, until they died of exposure or were killed by predatory beasts.

Several aspects of this are noteworthy. First, like most other ancient methods of execution, death by stoning was not instantaneous. Hanging or beheading are quick deaths; the guillotine, an extremely quick method, was introduced as a humane alternative to other practices, and as being more reliable than beheading with the sword. Compared to crucifixion or impalement, however, stoning was relatively quick; most victims would last only minutes, or perhaps an hour or so, but not many hours or days. It was, therefore, by the standards of the time, humane—though not as humane as beheading, or the Athenian practice of forcing the condemned person to drink hemlock juice.

Second, like other ancient methods, it was public. It is difficult to say whether this was intended as a deterrent for those observing the execution; it was perhaps meant to be humiliating, adding another layer of punishment to the pain and the certainty of death. Whatever the executioners may have intended, however, the human reality is that down through history public executions have been treated as a form of entertainment.

Third, stoning was in one way unlike many other methods: it had to be administered by a group. Sentence was passed on the basis of testimony from two or more (male) witnesses. Then all the mature men of the community were enjoined to carry out the penalty. This was regarded as a way of purging the group of the evil it had suffered, and which had contaminated it, from the crime that had been committed. As a practical matter, however, we should note that it meant that all who were involved in passing a sentence of death were, at least theoretically, also responsible for carrying it out.

What would a biblical system of criminal justice look like for us today, if we were to consider the proposal of the Christian Reconstructionists to follow the biblical model more closely in our legal system? In many cases it would mean simply overturning most of what we do now and beginning an entirely different method of punishment.

In the first place, we would have to abolish our entire prison system. In the ancient world, imprisonment as a punishment in itself was unknown; indeed, the logic of punishing someone by imprisonment would probably not have even been understood at the time. "Prisoners" were those awaiting trial or those captured in war, and such imprisonment was very brief: prisoners were killed, taken as booty (the young women and girls), enslaved (men and women), or returned to their homes on payment of tribute or ransom. No one, however, was held in captivity for a fixed term. No ancient society would have regarded it as a good, or even sane, use of resources to build a secure structure and pay people to guard it, as well as undertake the expense of feeding and other upkeep, simply to punish criminals.

In the New Testament, those in prison are usually those who are being held until they can be put on trial. For example, in Acts 12.1–5, Peter has been imprisoned by Herod (Agrippa), who intends to have him publicly punished when Passover has ended—in other words, after a few days. No long jail term is involved. In Acts 16.19–24, Paul and Silas are imprisoned (after being beaten) overnight, presumably until they can be expelled from the town of Philippi. Penalties, therefore, were of the sort that could be imposed and carried out expeditiously. Fines, mutilations, and executions all qualified on that score.

Adapting our system to this view of imprisonment would mean that jails would be reserved for those awaiting trial—and trial would need to follow swiftly on arrest, since lengthy jail time is not part of the biblical system. Overnight, or at most a few days, is what "jail" means in the Bible. No punishment could include sentencing to prison: life in prison without parole, or even prison terms of any duration at all, are not in the Bible. Our system of incarcerating millions of people for lengthy terms and employing hundreds of thousands to guard and feed them is not supported in any way by the Bible's practices. There is no biblical warrant for it.

Instead, we would have to come up with alternative punishments. There are four with biblical support: public beatings (with rods or whips, on the back, enough to draw blood but not to cause permanent injury); mutilation (cutting off the hand, for instance); fines or other monetary penalties (paid to the state or, more likely, to the injured party or parties); and death. The public beatings and mutilations would be carried out not merely to cause pain but also to humiliate the offender. Beatings were not only public, but also meant the offender was at least partially unclothed. And, as with the more recent punishment of being put in the stocks (that is, locked into a wooden restraint that immobilized one's hands and feet), while one was being beaten one was subject to gibes from the passing members of the public. Mutilation, in addition, was permanent, and one bore the mark of it therefore for life: a lost hand, facial disfigurement, or the like served as a public notice that one had been punished for a crime.

Financial penalties were primarily aimed at restitution. As such, they sometimes were the equivalent of civil penalties in our system of justice: a required payment to make someone else's loss whole. They also were meant to be a deterrent. In some cases (as with rape, for instance) they were used for crimes for which we would having difficulty considering such a penalty as sufficient.

We would also have to reconsider the kinds of crimes for which we would impose the death penalty. Except for deliberate murder and (if murder is involved) kidnapping, there is little overlap between the crimes for which the Bible imposes death and those we deem deserving of it, a list that includes working on the Sabbath (Exodus 31.14), cursing one's father and mother (Leviticus 20.9), committing adultery (Leviticus 20.10), and blaspheming the name of the Lord (Leviticus 24.16).

Even more adjustment would be necessary regarding the administration of the death penalty. For blasphemy, for example, the Bible requires the testimony of two witnesses to the commission of the sin, after which all the mature males—those making up "the community," the town—are *required* to participate in stoning the guilty person to death (Leviticus 24.14, 16). The requirement of two witnesses, of course, is to prevent false denunciations on the part of someone who holds a grudge or has some other ulterior motive for wishing to eliminate a fellow Israelite. The requirement that all mature males in the community participate in carrying out the penalty seems to have two rationales: if one is involved in condemning someone to death, one should be willing to impose the sentence; and, since the entire community has been shamed or polluted by the crime (blasphemy, in this case), the entire community must join in eliminating the source of pollution.

Clearly, the distance between what we think is a just system of punishment and what the Bible puts forth as necessary is vast. Those wishing to use the Bible as a warrant for imposing the death penalty will need to make a lot of adjustments—so many, in fact, that it would be fair to say that a biblical death penalty is not really the basis for the death penalty in modern societies. It is not simply a matter of saying that our ideas of punishment have changed; our very approach to what punishment is appropriate is essentially different from that of the Bible.

Take the punishment that differs the least from ours: imposing a financial penalty. We and the Bible agree that a fine is appropriate for such crimes as the destruction of property, like causing the death of livestock. (In our terms, this would cover such things as damage to one's automobile or home.) We do *not,* however, as the Bible does, include the rape of one's daughter as a crime of property (Deuteronomy 22.28–29). Restitution for such a crime, for us, would not mean paying a price to the victim's father, to make up to him for the loss of value in no longer having a virgin daughter to be married off.

In the case of mutilations for certain crimes, the vast majority of Americans would also find this beyond consideration. In fact, when such penalties are imposed in Islamic countries under Sharia law and they are reported in the Western media, they are often used as evidence that Islam is a primitive, vengeful religion. The same is true for public beatings, which we no longer use as a form of punishment but which are still imposed elsewhere.

That leaves the imposition of death for certain crimes. Here, our society and biblical society agree that this penalty is appropriate under some circumstances. (There are many who disagree with this practice, but we are trying to see on what basis we can continue a biblical practice, not on what basis we should discontinue it.) But we would differ sharply on the way it should be carried out.

We do not require all of the people in a community—or even all of the adult males—to participate in carrying out a sentence of death. Instead, we execute people in private, with only official witnesses. We deliberately aim for methods that do not cause pain. We do not regard the humiliation of the offender to be an essential part of the punishment. Our executions are no longer public events that many people watch or participate in. Among many other reasons for our change of attitude about public execution is that we believe that it coarsens people's sensibilities to watch such things.

The history of lynching in this country should have made us all aware how easy it is, under the cover of supporting justice, to carry out vengeful slayings that are not based on evidence of wrongdoing. (We can see the same phenomenon in Numbers 14.1–10, where because the people fear that in trying to conquer the land they themselves will be conquered, they are at the point of turning into a mob and stoning Moses, Aaron, Joshua, and Caleb.) It is therefore not surprising that in the modern world we have not adopted a model of capital punishment that relies on the actions of a group in order to carry it out. But an attempt to implement the biblical norm—that any execution be carried out by the entire community—would have to take the reasons for such a practice into account. Essentially, in the biblical view, a capital crime committed by a member of the community damages the entire community, and therefore the entire community must participate in the punishment so that the evil of the perpetrator can be purged.

What would implementing a biblical view of the death penalty mean for us today? First, for most if not virtually all Americans, the option of reinstituting the practice of communal executions is simply unthinkable, no matter what the Bible says. Besides the possibility of reviving the practice of lynchings, and even if executions only followed duly conducted trials, many or most members of the "community," whatever it might be, would not wish to kill someone personally. Those who would wish to do so, on the other hand—like those who volunteer for firing squads—might be exactly the kind of vengeful people whom it would be unwise to encourage.

It might be feasible, however, to mandate a public referendum on the death penalty at set periods. In other words, those states that still maintain the death penalty for certain crimes would have to renew that legal practice periodically, and not by action of the legislature but by vote of the state's population. In other words, the residents of the state would have to go on record in support of their state's use of the death penalty. Alternatively, instead of periodic votes, a vote could be mandated every time someone on death row was exonerated by new evidence. In this case, those supporting the continuance of the death penalty would have to obtain a new mandate for it if it had been shown that one person had been unjustly convicted of a capital crime.

One other area of our criminal justice system that we might want to reexamine, under the influence of biblical practice, is that of lengthy imprisonments for all sorts of crimes. Certain crimes, like petty theft or fraud, we might want to shift into the restitution column: if convicted, you must repay your victims or you must be under a court order to turn over some proportion of your income to a fund that reimburses those victimized by fraud. Other crimes, like substance abuse, could be better addressed by treatment programs than by imprisonment. A civilian labor corps, undertaking public works such as road repair, reforestation, or other necessary activities, could be something that convicted criminals could be sentenced to carry out. At the very least, we would vastly reduce the proportion of our population that was incarcerated at any given time: only the most violent inmates, or those who had definitively shown that they could not be rehabilitated, would remain. Inmates who were very ill or very old could be released on demonstration that they truly posed no further threat of harm to anyone.

So what could we say to those who wish to impose a biblical criminal code today? One response is to affirm that we have progressed beyond the Bible in moral insight about punishment, but to acknowledge that with careful consideration we can derive a good deal of insight from what the Bible says about punishment and apply it, with profit, to our own situation. We do not, by and large, regard public humiliation—crucifixion, stoning, whipping, caning, or even such relatively minor punishments as being put in the stocks or being made to wear a dunce cap—as appropriate forms of punishment. We do not accept the word of two witnesses as sufficient for the imposition of death. We do not think that blasphemy or gluttony, though they may be wrong, deserve to be punished by death.

Most importantly, we do not try to force our secular penal codes to institute biblical norms. We do not accept the idea that the entire community must carry out the sentence of death, though we may consider ways in which we can periodically bring the community to reconsider whether that is what it wants to do. We do not even force jurors who have imposed a death sentence to carry it out themselves. Why do we not do this? We may suspect that jurors would be reluctant to sentence people to death if they themselves had to carry out the sentence. Yet such a practice, carried out in public, would be far closer to biblical norms than what we have today: either no death sentences at all, in jurisdictions that have ended the death penalty, or "private" executions, not open to the public, carried out by hired professionals in front of official witnesses.

We are sensitive to the need to guard against inflaming vengefulness. We are aware in numerous ways of how easy it is to be mistaken, and so we guard against error in capital trials (though in some areas our record shows that we are not on guard enough). In other words, we have advanced beyond the Bible's moral grasp of punishment. To put the Bible's standards in this area into practice would be a step backwards, a moral devolution.

Biblical Economics?

In June of 2002, the Southern Baptist Convention passed a resolution at their convention in St. Louis that affirmed "Christian counseling that relies upon the Word of God rather than theories that are rooted in a defective understanding of human nature." * The goal of this resolution was to counter a "therapeutic" culture that relied on secular theories of mental health rather than the principles—including "obedience to Holy Scripture," "the redemptive work of Christ and the sanctifying power of the Holy Spirit through the Word of God"—that are to be derived entirely from the Bible.

In a statement accompanying the decision of Southern Baptist Theological Seminary to change its entire counseling program to one based solely on biblical principles, Dean Russell Moore of the school of theology stated, "You can't simply say you're going to integrate the science of psychotherapy with scripture because there are only sciences and theories of psychotherapy that are contradictory and incoherent."[†]

Suppose that instead of, or in addition to, revising their view of pastoral counseling, the Southern Baptists had also proposed to revise their view of how the economy should work, and how biblical principles should infuse both theories of economics and the behavior of ordinary Christians? Suppose that the Convention had passed a resolution saying, "We affirm an understanding of Christian economics that relies upon the Word of God rather than upon theories that are rooted in a defective understanding of human nature"? What if the dean of the school of theology had said that Southern Seminary would henceforth instruct its graduates in biblical economics rather than in secular "sciences of economics that are contradictory and incoherent"? Would they be able to carry out their plan?

It would actually be easier to come up with a "biblical economics" than it is to come up with a "biblical therapy." The Bible is quite clear on the basic matters involved: essentially, wealth should be distributed more or less equally among all of

---

* The complete text may be found at the Southern Baptist Convention's website: www.sbc.net/resolutions/amResolution.asp?ID=1119.
† David Winfrey, "Biblical Therapy," *The Christian Century* (January 23, 2007), 24–27.

the people of the community, and, failing that, the community as a whole should make sure that the poorest among them have access to the basic necessities of life.

On the matter of redistribution of property, the commandment is outlined in Leviticus 25.1–55. Every fiftieth year, all property returns to its original owner—in other words, the distribution that was carried out at the time of the conquest of the land will be reinstated.

> You shall count off seven weeks of years, seven times seven years, so that the period of seven weeks of years gives forty-nine years. Then you shall have the trumpet sounded loud; on the tenth day of the seventh month—on the day of atonement—you shall have the trumpet sounded throughout all your land. And you shall hallow the fiftieth year and you shall proclaim liberty throughout the land to all its inhabitants. It shall be a jubilee for you: you shall return, every one of you, to your property and every one of you to your family. . . .
>
> The land shall not be sold in perpetuity, for the land is mine [i.e., the LORD's]; with me you are but aliens and tenants. Throughout the land that you hold, you shall provide for the redemption of the land.
>
> If anyone of your kin falls into difficulty and sells a piece of property, . . . what was sold shall remain with the purchaser until the year of jubilee; in the jubilee it shall be released, and the property shall be returned. (Leviticus 25.8–10, 23–25, 28)

In the New Testament this principle is restated, first by Jesus in his encounter with the rich ruler (Mark 10.17–22 and parallels): "Sell what you own, and give the money to the poor." It is then carried out, to the extent possible, in the early Christian community, as explained in Acts 2.44–45: "All who believed were together and had all things in common; they would sell their possessions and goods and distribute the proceeds to all, as any had need."

These principles are in stark contrast to the practices of modern capitalist economies, which create huge disparities of wealth (and perpetuate them) and which, in the United States at least, do not provide such basics as guaranteed health care, medicine, or shelter for poor citizens. In addition, in following the practices of modern capitalism, the United States is carrying out an economic philosophy that is, in the words of the Southern Baptists, "rooted in a defective understanding of human nature." Capitalism as currently practiced sees human beings as essentially economic actors who are trying to maximize their individual wealth and their control of resources. It does not treat human beings as members of a larger group, cooperating on matters of mutual benefit. And it certainly has no place for any ideas of redemption, acknowledgment of sin, or reparation of goods to those who have been less fortunate.

As many observers have noted, disparities of wealth in the United States today are at their highest levels since the 1920s. The top 1 percent of earners bring home more than 20 percent of the income; the bottom 20 percent bring home around 14 percent. The *average* CEO of a Fortune 500 company makes nearly $14 million a year, and some heads of hedge funds make *billions* of dollars a year. Meanwhile, over forty million Americans have no health insurance; tens of millions of people, including millions of children, live below the poverty level; and millions have inadequate shelter, or no shelter at all. These facts have been extensively reported, in various media, but the general response runs along lines such as, "This is what happens in a capitalist economy. There's nothing we can do about it."

But is that the case? Is there nothing a Christian can do as an actor in this economy? The biblical answer seems clear enough: work to assure, in the near term, that all members of the community have at least the minimum necessary for supporting life (food and shelter); and, over the longer term, that disparities of wealth are at least greatly reduced. It would therefore seem to be the duty of those who hold out the Bible as the moral guide for life to support provision of health insurance to all people, to promote tax policies that provide enough money to run effective poverty programs, to provide enough income support to lift families with children above the poverty line, and so on.

The Bible also speaks clearly about indebtedness:

Every seventh year you shall grant a remission of debts. And
this is the manner of the remission: every creditor shall remit
the claim that is held against a neighbor, not exacting it of a
neighbor who is a member of the community, because the
LORD's remission has been proclaimed. Of a foreigner you
may exact it, but you must remit your claim on whatever any
member of your community owes you. There will, however,
be no one in need among you, because the LORD is sure to
bless you in the land that the LORD your God is giving you as
a possession to occupy, if only you will obey the LORD your
God by diligently observing this entire commandment that I
command you today. When the LORD your God has blessed
you, as he promised you, you will lend to many nations, but
you will not borrow; you will rule over many nations, but
they will not rule over you. (Deuteronomy 15.1–6)

Thus any loan outstanding during the seventh, Sabbatarian year
is to be forgiven completely, and everyone is to start afresh.
Implementation of such a rule in the current U.S. economy
would certainly be complex, but those advocating for the Bible
as the absolute guide to moral behavior need to explain how
they would deal with matters such as these.

It is not a sufficient objection to this view that the Bible
shows such economic practice being carried out in communities where everyone was an adherent of the religious beliefs on
which the economic view was based. The point is not whether
this could be done in today's society—it is very difficult to imagine, for example, the redistribution on egalitarian economic lines
of all the real estate in the United States—but rather what is
being held up for us as an ideal. Even if we do not go so far as
to try and model our economic life on the jubilee year, or the
remission of all debt every seventh year, there are plenty of other
passages that mandate allocation of resources from the well-off
to those less fortunate. For example, Leviticus 23.22 states,
"When you reap the harvest of your land, you shall not reap to
the very edges of your field, or gather the gleanings of your harvest; you shall leave them for the poor and for the alien." In the

New Testament we have Jesus exhorting his followers to give food to the hungry and clothing to the naked, and implying (at least) that their salvation depends on having done such things (Matthew 25.31–46). The letter of James says, "If a brother or sister is naked and lacks daily food, and one of you says to them, 'Go in peace; keep warm and eat your fill,' and yet you do not supply their bodily needs, what is the good of that?" (2.15–16).

It is not simply on the matter of the distribution of wealth that the Bible might stand in judgment over our current practices. Consider the following regulation (Note: the "pledge" referred to in this passage is whatever property of the borrower is put up as guarantee of repayment of a loan):

> When you make your neighbor a loan of any kind, you shall not go into the house to take the pledge. You shall wait outside, while the person to whom you are making the loan brings the pledge out to you. If the person is poor, you shall not sleep in [the garment given to you as] the pledge. You shall give the pledge back by sunset, so that your neighbor may sleep in the cloak and bless you. (Deuteronomy 24.10–13) [The bracketed words in the NRSV translation are supplied; they are not in the original.]

The point of this regulation is as follows. It is legal to take possession of someone's property as guarantee that they will repay a loan. (Pawnbrokers, in other words, are biblical.) If, however, the property is the person's only outer garment—and the clear implication of the passage is that the person has no house—the pledge may not be kept, but must be handed back *no later than that evening* so that the person has some protection from the cold while sleeping. If the underlying principle of this rule were applied to our situation today—that it is unjust to deprive anyone, no matter whether they are a debtor to us or not, of necessary shelter—it would be illegal to foreclose on a mortgage and turn families out of their houses if they had nowhere else to live.

Another, related regulation might also have relevance in our day. Deuteronomy 24.6 says, "No one shall take a mill or an upper millstone in pledge, for that would be taking a life in pledge." Taking an entire grain mill, or even the upper stone, would mean that the miller could not grind any grain. It would effectively be depriving him of his livelihood. Similarly, in our economy, we could make it illegal to repossess an automobile from someone who fell behind on car payments, if the automobile were essential to the livelihood of the person. In some cases, at least, a person without an automobile cannot get to work, and often cannot get to stores to shop for food.

One final matter should be of interest to us in these economic regulations: those rules that deal with aliens living within the borders of Israel. Here are three instances:

> You shall not deprive a resident alien or an orphan of justice.... When you reap your harvest in the field and forget a sheaf in the field, you shall not go back to get it; it shall be left for the alien, the orphan, and the widow.... Remember that you were a slave in the land of Egypt; therefore I am commanding you to do this. (Deuteronomy 24.17, 19, 22)

> When an alien resides with you in your land, you shall not oppress the alien. The alien who resides with you shall be to you as the citizen among you; you shall love the alien as yourself, for you were aliens in the land of Egypt. (Leviticus 19.33–34)

> There shall be for both you and the resident alien a single statute, a perpetual statute throughout your generations; you and the alien shall be alike before the LORD. You and the alien who resides with you shall have the same law and the same ordinance. (Numbers 15.15–16)

The Bible clearly does not want to make a hard distinction between citizens and aliens, to the disadvantage of the latter. The Israelites are to remember that they were oppressed aliens in a foreign land, and, remembering that, they are to refrain from treating anyone else as they were treated. This can provide guidance for those thinking about the issue of immigrants in the United States, since (other than Native Americans, who presumably migrated into this area before any other human inhabitants) every single person now resident in the United States either came here from elsewhere or is descended from someone who migrated here.

The Bible is very straightforward on relations between the different classes of society (primarily viewed in economic terms): don't favor the rich.

> Alas for those who are at ease in Zion,
>   and for those who feel secure on Mount Samaria,
> the notables of the first of the nations,
>   to whom the house of Israel resorts! . . .
> Alas for those who lie on beds of ivory,
>   and lounge on their couches,
> and eat lambs from the flock,
>   and calves from the stall;
> who sing idle songs to the sound of the harp,
>   and like David improvise on instruments of music;
> who drink wine from bowls,
>   and anoint themselves with the finest oils,
>   but are not grieved over the ruin of Joseph!
> Therefore they shall now be the first to go into exile,
>   and the revelry of the loungers shall pass away.
>
> (Amos 6.1, 4–7)

There are many such passages in the prophets. In the New Testament, the letter of James can serve as an example:

> If any think they are religious, and do not bridle their tongues but deceive their hearts, their religion is worthless. Religion that is pure and undefiled before God, the Father, is this: to care for orphans and widows in their distress, and to keep oneself unstained by the world.
>
> My brothers and sisters, do you with your acts of favoritism really believe in our glorious Lord Jesus Christ? For if a person with gold rings and in fine clothes comes into your assembly, and if a poor person in dirty clothes also comes in, and if you take notice of the one wearing the fine clothes and say, "Have a seat here, please," while to the one who is

poor you say, "Stand there," or "Sit at my feet" [*literally* "Sit
under my footstool"], have you not made distinctions among
yourselves, and become judges with evil thoughts? Listen, my
beloved brothers and sisters. Has not God chosen the poor in
the world to be rich in faith and to be heirs of the kingdom
that he has promised to those who love him? But you have
dishonored the poor. Is it not the rich who oppress you? Is it
not they who drag you into court? Is it not they who
blaspheme the excellent name that was invoked over you?
(James 1.26–2.7)

As a partial antidote to such passages, Leviticus has an interesting command: "You shall not render an unjust judgment; you
shall not be partial to the poor or defer to the great: with justice
you shall judge your neighbor" (19.15). This may be the only
place—it is the only one I can find—where it is made explicit
that favoritism toward the poor in matters of justice is not
allowed. But this does not amount to much of a concession
toward the rich. In the biblical communities, as in most of the
world, the problem was almost never favoritism toward the poor.
If the justice system worked impartially no matter who appeared
before it—if poor people had top-flight legal representation; if
they had the resources to appeal to higher courts, to engage in
delaying tactics (and if they had the income to survive while
such delays played themselves out); if they truly could compete
with the wealthy on an equal footing in our courts of law—we
could then turn our attention to seeing whether they were in
fact being treated too favorably. Right now, however, that does
not seem to be a problem among us.

In the matter of providing money for government programs
that aid poor and unfortunate people—legal aid, welfare, health
care for the indigent, disability payments, and so on—people will
sometimes argue that in the Bible this was a matter for private
charity and should not therefore be carried out by general tax-
ation over the entire population. Whatever the actual practices in
the biblical communities, however, the laws (as noted above)
required that wealthy farmers not reap all their crops, but leave

some in every field to be gathered by the destitute. In addition, if debts were to be forgiven and all property redistributed on a regular basis, such practices would actually be *more* thoroughgoing than our tax code today. Tithes were also a requirement: according to Deuteronomy 12.6, once the Temple had been established, the Israelites were to "go there, bringing there your burnt offerings and your sacrifices, your tithes and your donations, your votive gifts, your freewill offerings, and the firstlings of your herds and flocks." We should note that these offerings at the Temple are *in addition* to taxes that Solomon and his successors would have been levying on the population.

Finally, on the larger issue of political rights and responsibilities—beyond the matter of economic justice—the Bible does have a position on whether the head of state must obey the laws of the state.

> When [the king] has taken the throne of his kingdom, he shall have a copy of this law written for him in the presence of the levitical priests. It shall remain with him and he shall read in it all the days of his life, so that he may learn to fear the LORD his God, diligently observing all the words of this law and these statutes, neither exalting himself above other members of the community nor turning aside from the commandment, either to the right or to the left, so that he and his descendants may reign long over his kingdom in Israel. (Deuteronomy 17.18–20)

The requirement that the law should be written "in the presence of the levitical priests," who were the upholders of the legal traditions, would correspond to something like "under the supervision of the Supreme Court" in our terms. But the main purport of this passage should be clear. To the question of whether the king is above the law or subject to the law, the Bible responds unambiguously: the king is subject to the law. The king is a member of the community like other members, and must uphold the entirety of the law while observing it himself. The king does not make law.

As we have seen, the biblical link between justice and righteousness is very strong and clear. And righteousness is a social phenomenon, not merely a private, individual one. It is not good
enough, in the biblical view, to be upright and moral in one's private life, but then to act unjustly when one enters the public sphere
or operates a business. Righteousness—including justice for the
least well-off among one's fellow-citizens, and for foreigners living among us—is an obligation that must be carried out throughout one's activities. And achieving justice is not just a matter of
criminal law and trials. It involves the entirety of society, the fair
distribution of all resources across all income groups, and the provision of sufficient food and shelter for everyone to survive.

The point of linking criminal justice with social and economic justice is to clarify that in the biblical view, these are not
separated in any sense. There is no such thing as a biblical "law
and order" approach that only deals with criminal matters and
does not have something to say about the basic fairness of the
wider social network. The laws dealing with all of these matters
are completely intertwined. It may very well be that we see,
thanks to our greater experience in economic matters and the
complexity of the modern, industrial and postindustrial world,
that an unimaginative application of biblical strictures simply
would not work in America, Western Europe, and other
advanced economies. That is a legitimate argument. But as we
shall also see, advancing such an argument makes it much more
difficult to advocate for the simple application of other biblical
laws in other areas of life. Justice requires us to acknowledge that
if we, in our modern sophistication, loosen the biblical laws
about income fairness, for example, we cannot complain when
others, following modern psychological understandings of sexuality, or modern social understandings of the abilities of women,
refuse to apply specific biblical strictures to the regulation of sexual morality or to the determination of what roles women may
and may not take on in today's world. "Fair is fair," as kids say.

5

SLAVES, WOMEN, AND JEWS

What Does the Bible Say about "Those People"?

DO YOU THINK that you, or your cash-strapped neighbor, or any other father with money problems should be allowed to sell his daughter to the highest bidder? The Bible seems to think that that is a perfectly good way to deal with one's economic difficulties. Should we allow this?

For that matter, do you think that neighbor himself should be subject to involuntary servitude if he cannot pay off his debts? The Bible seems to think that it is fine to enslave someone under those circumstances. Is that how we should get someone to pay off his credit cards or his bank overdraft?

Do you think your neighbor's wife is at the top of his list of possessions? Do you think finding her sexually attractive, and wishing she were your wife, is the same thing as wishing his Mercedes, or his luxurious McMansion, were yours? That seems to be the way the Bible looks at things. Is that how we should look at them as well?

Do you think Jews are descended from Satan, or at the least, that they follow a satanic religion? The Bible seems to be telling us just that. Is that how we should think?

These sorts of questions can help us look specifically at some topics on which Christians have disagreed in the past, all the

78

while claiming to look to the Bible as an authority in their lives. They will also reveal some of the different ways we have approached the contradictions within Scripture, and have changed our attitudes toward slavery, the status of women, and the place of Jews in the Christian scheme of salvation.

Parts of the Bible speak ill of women and Jews, and some passages support, or at least condone, slavery. Other passages mitigate—perhaps even contradict—some of the harsh passages. So what should we do? Put the passages up against each other, and pick the one that's closest to what we really think nowadays? How exactly is that using the Bible for guidance? What that would really amount to is finding parts of the Bible that jibe as closely as possible with what we already believe, and choosing them not as the basis for our beliefs, but as validation for the beliefs we formed elsewhere. So what approach to these contradictory passages should we take?

Slavery

Nowhere in the Bible is slavery expressly forbidden. It is certainly regulated in many ways, and slaves have rights; slavery can be brought to an end, either by prearrangement between the parties or by legal requirement. And by the time of the letter to Philemon, it is clear that at least in Paul's mind, slaves who have become Christians should be treated as equals within the Christian community, even by their masters. He does not claim that slaves should be set free, but he does provide a theological basis for making that claim. Nevertheless, they should not, he argues elsewhere (1 Corinthians 7.21–24), try to free themselves on their own. Everyone should remain in the social position that they were in at the time they became Christian—the momentousness of that decision and its consequences completely dwarf any other aspects of one's life.

First, we can look at a couple of passages in which slave regulations are given. In Exodus we read:

> When you buy a male Hebrew slave, he shall serve six years,
> but in the seventh he shall go out a free person, without debt.

> If he comes in single, he shall go out single; if he comes in
> married, then his wife shall go out with him. If his master
> gives him a wife and she bears him sons or daughters, the
> wife and her children shall be her master's and he shall go out
> alone. But if the slave declares, "I love my master, my wife, and
> my children; I will not go out a free person," then his master
> shall bring him before God. He shall be brought to the door
> or the doorpost; and his master shall pierce his ear with an
> awl; and he shall serve him for life. (21.2–6)

In the first part of this passage we see that Hebrew slaves were
not at all in the same category as were slaves in the United States
before the Civil War, or for that matter as were serfs in feudal
Europe or in Russia before their emancipation. In the United
States slavery was based on race and slaves were in bondage for
life, with virtually no possibility of becoming free except by their
owners' consent. This is sometimes called "chattel slavery." In the
Bible, what is presented in such passages is more like indentured
servitude, where someone agrees to labor for another with no
recompense other than food and lodging because of indebtedness or because his own means of support have vanished (if, for
instance, he lost his ancestral land). Here in Exodus it is made
clear that such servitude cannot last more than six years; in the
Sabbath year such a servant must be set free.

There is an important caveat, however: if during the slave's
time of service his master provided him with a wife (presumably
herself a slave) and that wife bore children, the wife and children
remain the master's property. The male slave is therefore faced
with the choice of freedom but with the loss of his family, or else
lifelong enslavement while remaining with his family. This must
have been, at least some of the time, a painful choice.

Physical abuse of slaves is legally limited, but not prohibited
entirely:

> When a slaveowner strikes a male or female slave with a rod
> and the slave dies immediately, the owner shall be punished.
> But if the slave survives a day or two, there is no punishment;
> for the slave is the owner's property. (Exodus 21.20–21)

> When a slaveowner strikes the eye of a male or female slave,
> destroying it, the owner shall let the slave go, a free person, to
> compensate for the eye. If the owner knocks out a tooth of a
> male or female slave, the slave shall be let go, a free person, to
> compensate for the tooth. (Exodus 21.26–27)

Depending on which of these strictures we give more weight to, we can read the regulations regarding slaves as either tending toward treating them as property or tending toward treating them as fully human beings. This is also clear in the laws relating to the treatment of female Israelite slaves, including daughters:

> When a man sells his daughter as a slave, she shall not go out
> as the male slaves do. If she does not please her master, who
> designated her for himself, then he shall let her be redeemed;
> he shall have no right to sell her to a foreign people, since he
> has dealt unfairly with her. If he designates her for his son, he
> shall deal with her as with a daughter. If he takes another wife
> to himself, he shall not diminish the food, clothing, or marital
> rights of the first wife. And if he does not do these three
> things for her, she shall go out without debt, without payment
> of money. (Exodus 21.7–11)

A daughter sold to another Israelite so that her father can get out of debt has the right to be treated as a wife would be if obtained in any other way (or as a recognized daughter-in-law if she was purchased for a son). Unlike slaves captured in war, she cannot be sold out of the country. She is not to be made to go out and work in the fields. In fact, this situation differs little from one in which a daughter is betrothed to a man and the man pays a bride-price to the father. The exigencies of the father's economic situation may limit him and his daughter in a number of ways, but they do not erase all of her rights in the matter.

In later Israelite legal codes (those in Deuteronomy), attitudes have evolved somewhat in the direction of supporting the full humanity of slaves:

> Slaves who have escaped to you from their owners shall not
> be given back to them. They shall reside with you, in your
> midst, in any place they choose in any one of your towns,
> wherever they please; you shall not oppress them.
> (Deuteronomy 23.15–16)

> If a member of your community, whether a Hebrew man or a
> Hebrew woman, is sold to you and works for you six years, in
> the seventh year you shall set that person free. And when you
> send a male slave out from you a free person, you shall not
> send him out empty-handed. Provide liberally out of your
> flock, your threshing floor, and your wine press, thus giving to
> him some of the bounty with which the LORD your God has
> blessed you. Remember that you were a slave in the land of
> Egypt, and the LORD your God redeemed you; for this reason
> I lay this command on you today. (Deuteronomy 15.12–15)

> Remember that you were a slave in Egypt. (Deuteronomy
> 16.12)

> Remember that you were a slave in Egypt. . . . Remember
> that you were a slave in the land of Egypt. (Deuteronomy
> 24.18, 22)

The repetition that escaped slaves should be free to live anywhere, and the constant reminders of Israel's experience of being
slaves themselves, serve to reinforce the argument that slaves must
at least be treated humanely, and that they are no different from
other Israelites.

In the New Testament, slavery is more or less taken for
granted as a social institution and there is no attempt to develop
laws for it, since the New Testament writers were not thinking
of setting up their own commonwealth. In the gospels, slaves
appear or are mentioned along with other social types—soldiers,
priests, shepherds, and so on. Jesus heals the slave of the centu-
rion (Matthew 8.5–13 and parallels); Peter in the garden of
Gethsemane takes a sword and attacks the group that had come
to arrest Jesus, cutting off the ear of the high priest's slave (John
18.10; in Mark 14.47 and Luke 22.50 the one who attacks the

slave is not named). But slavery is also used metaphorically; thus, Jesus says to his followers: "Whoever wishes to be first among you must be slave of all" (Mark 10.44).

The same holds true with the treatment of slavery in the letters of Paul and others. Slavery is a fact of life, and some members of the community were, or had been, slaves: "Were you a slave when called [to join the community]?" Paul asks (1 Corinthians 7.21). "There is no longer Jew or Greek, there is no longer slave or free, there is no longer male and female; for all of you are one in Christ Jesus," he states in Galatians 3.28, clearly indicating that slavery is a category of human existence like gender or nationality. In the "household codes," those portions in some of the New Testament letters dealing with the rules by which domestic life should be governed, slavery is one social arrangement among others, such as marriage and parenthood:

> Slaves, obey your earthly masters with fear and trembling, in singleness of heart, as you obey Christ; not only while being watched, and in order to please them, but as slaves of Christ, doing the will of God from the heart. Render service with enthusiasm, as to the Lord and not to men and women, knowing that whatever good we do, we will receive the same again from the Lord, whether we are slaves or free. And, masters, do the same to them. Stop threatening them, for you know that both of you have the same Master in heaven, and with him there is no partiality. (Ephesians 6.5–9)

Here, though, in addition to the social reality of slavery, we see the beginnings of the use of slavery as a metaphor for one's service to God through Christ. The passage from 1 Corinthians above, after referring to actual servitude, goes on to say: "For whoever was called in the Lord as a slave is a freed person belonging to the Lord, just as whoever was free when called is a slave of Christ" (7.22).

This provides a basis for arguing, as the experience of the Israelites as slaves in Egypt did, that Christians should regard slaves as their equals, since the call to be Christian is far more important than the social relationship between master and slave.

It also indicates that in fact both those who are free and those who are slaves share a common humanity. In Paul's letter to Philemon, in fact, this seems to be the main point. Though the situation that gave rise to the letter is not entirely clear, it seems that the slave Onesimus has fled from his master Philemon and has come under Paul's protection. Either before that time, or during the time he was with Paul, Onesimus became a Christian. Paul is now sending him back to Philemon, who had himself become a Christian under Paul's guidance. Thus Paul exhorts Philemon to receive Onesimus as "a beloved brother" and to "welcome him as you would welcome me" (vv. 16, 17)—a strong indication of Paul's belief that the fellowship of Christians should overcome these traditional social barriers.

It is in the Book of Revelation that we find perhaps the strongest implied condemnation of slave trading in the New Testament:

> "Alas, alas, the great city,
>   Babylon, the mighty city!
> For in one hour your judgment has come!"
> And the merchants of the earth weep and mourn for her,
> since no one buys their cargo anymore, cargo of gold, silver,
> jewels and pearls, fine linen, purple, silk and scarlet, all kinds
> of scented wood, all articles of ivory, all articles of costly
> wood, bronze, iron, and marble, cinnamon, spice, incense,
> myrrh, frankincense, wine, olive oil, choice flour and wheat,
> cattle and sheep, horses and chariots, slaves—and human lives.
>   (18.10–13)

Few New Testament passages make clearer the link between luxury goods and human exploitation. And the images of the destruction of "Babylon" (the book's code word for Rome) make clear the utter condemnation of the commercial and imperial power of Rome. Since the economy of the ancient world depended in part on slave labor, the author of the Revelation is pointing out that the luxurious lifestyles of the rich depend on traffic not just in luxury goods but in human lives.

Women

When we turn to the topic of women in the Bible, we are faced with a variety of attitudes, some very negative and others less so. In the Book of Ecclesiasticus, or the Wisdom of Jesus ben Sirach (which is part of the Roman Catholic and Orthodox canons but not the Protestant Bible), we have what is probably the most extreme view of women presented in any biblical text:

> Better is the wickedness of a man
> > than a woman who does good;
> > it is woman who brings shame and disgrace. (42.14)

Nonetheless, all Christians (Orthodox, Catholic, and Protestant) can point to this passage from 1 Timothy:

> But refuse to put younger widows on the list [of those who would be supported by the community]; for when their sensual desires alienate them from Christ, they want to marry, and so they incur condemnation for having violated their first pledge [to live a life of prayer]. Besides that, they learn to be idle, gadding about from house to house; and they are not merely idle, but also gossips and busybodies, saying what they should not say. So I would have younger widows marry, bear children, and manage their households, so as to give the adversary no occasion to revile us. For some have already turned away to follow Satan. (5.11–15)

Anyone familiar with gender stereotypes will recognize this one: the flighty, lusty, empty-headed young woman with not enough to do, who fills up her days with scandal and gossip, who needs a husband to control her, and who ought to have housework and children to keep her busy and out of mischief. And there is this, from the Book of Proverbs:

> Like a gold ring in a pig's snout
> > is a beautiful woman without good sense. (11.22)

There is no comparable proverb characterizing handsome but brainless men (though such beings *do* exist), just as there is no denunciation in a New Testament letter of men who are idle gossips.

A more subtle point, not obvious in English translations of the Bible, is due to the gendered character of Hebrew verbs. The Ten Commandments (Exodus 20.1–17; Deuteronomy 5.6–21) are addressed to males (they are second-person masculine singular in form). That is perhaps why the final commandment, against covetousness, enumerates the possessions of the neighbor that must not be coveted: his house, his wife, his male or female slave, his ox, his donkey, or any other property that is his. The "house" probably means the entirety of his household, not specifically the building in which he lives; but the enumeration that follows is intended to draw out the meaning of what the neighbor's household consists of. At the top of the list of possessions is the woman.

The Bible is, therefore, both slanted and limited in its view of women. But there are texts that counter this prevailing view and balance some of the more extreme passages on the other side. We have already noted the law that punishes a rapist by exacting a monetary penalty, to be paid to the father of the victim, and that forces the rapist to marry his victim (Deuteronomy 22.23–29). The coldness and cruelty of this law toward the victim—though part of its aim is to make sure that she has a husband, in a society where an unmarried woman is a vulnerable being—is countered by the harrowing and heartrending account of the rape of Tamar by her half-brother, Amnon (2 Samuel 13.1–39), which is part of the narrative of the domestic turmoil during King David's reign. Amnon was obsessed with Tamar's great beauty— in fact, he is a classic instance of a male predator who "was so tormented that he made himself ill because of his [half-]sister Tamar" (v. 2). By a ploy he got her alone in his room, and then forced her to have intercourse with him. As soon as he had forced her, the account says, he

> was seized with a very great loathing for her; indeed, his
> loathing was even greater than the lust he had felt for her.
> Amnon said to her, "Get out!" But she said to him, "No, my

> brother; for this wrong in sending me away is greater than the
> other you did to me." But he would not listen to her. He
> called the young man who served him and said, "Put this
> woman out of my presence, and bolt the door after her."
> (Now she was wearing a long robe with sleeves; for this is
> how the virgin daughters of the king were clothed in earlier
> times.) So his servant put her out, and bolted the door after
> her. But Tamar put ashes on her head, and tore the long robe
> that she was wearing; she put her hand on her head, and went
> away, crying aloud as she went. (2 Samuel 13:15–19)

The narrator here clearly expresses and evokes great sympathy
for Tamar, even though the main point of this account is to
explain the disarray in King David's household and the complicated events that will come to a head when he is dying. The
piteous irony of Tamar herself tearing the garment that symbolized her modesty and innocence, just as those qualities themselves have been torn from her, is hard to miss. And we should
note that she calls on Amnon to carry out the demands of the
law and marry her, though he disregards his obligation; the failure of David to act in the matter essentially allows him, as the
king's oldest son, to escape any punishment. Amnon's great sin is
compounded by David's weak acquiescence in it.

We have already noted above Paul's statement in the letter to
the Galatians (3.28) that Christ has abolished the barriers and
inequalities of gender just as he has abolished those of nationality and social status. This counters later statements in other New
Testament letters that are efforts to maintain or reassert a second-
class status for women in the Christian community. In 1 Timothy the writer says:

> I desire, then, that in every place the men should pray, lifting
> up holy hands without anger or argument; also that the
> women should dress themselves modestly and decently in
> suitable clothing, not with their hair braided, or with gold,
> pearls, or expensive clothes, but with good works, as is proper
> for women who profess reverence for God. Let a woman
> learn in silence with full submission. I permit no woman to

teach or to have authority over a man; she is to keep silent. For Adam was formed first, then Eve; and Adam was not deceived, but the woman was deceived and became a transgressor. Yet she will be saved through childbearing, provided they continue in faith and love and holiness, with modesty. (2.8–15)

The concern with female modesty, with keeping women silent and in their places, with the emphasis on bearing children as the means by which women can be redeemed from the burden of the first sinner, Eve, and with strictures against any female authority over any male are all aspects of gender relations that continue in some places right down to the present day. We can merely note that the text itself is evidence that women did teach and hold authoritative positions at least in some communities, perhaps even preaching or speaking in public, since otherwise these prohibitions would not have been necessary.

The Jews
With regard to the New Testament's treatment of Jews, many Christians are now aware that the charge of anti-Semitism has been leveled at some of the texts. (Since the passages in question are not based on racial or ethnic character but rather reflect religious differences, many writers prefer to call this "anti-Judaism" rather than anti-Semitism.) There are places where Jews or Judaism are treated negatively or as a foil for positive characterizations of the new Christian community in its separation from Judaism. Some of these texts are extremely problematic for Christians today. In Matthew's narrative of the events leading up to Jesus' crucifixion, a crowd of Jews calls on Pilate to crucify Jesus. Pilate's response is to wash his hands and declare himself innocent of guilt for putting Jesus to death, since it is the crowd that wants the death. "Then the people as a whole answered, 'His blood be on us and on our children!'" (Matthew 27.25). This cry of "blood guilt," as it came to be known, was used for centuries by Christians to justify persecution and execution of Jews.

In the letters of Paul, the theological approach becomes more nuanced. In Galatians 4.21–5.1, Paul develops his idea of the relationship between Judaism (the religion of those who are "enslaved" to the law) and Christianity (the religion of faith in God and the promise to Abraham that preceded the giving of the law on Sinai). To do this he allegorizes the two sons of Abraham, Ishmael (the son of Hagar, a slave) and Isaac (the son of Sarah, a free woman). In an interpretation that would surely strike any Jew, then or now, as perverse, Paul identifies Jews with the child of Hagar and Christians, many of whom were by now Gentiles, with the child of Sarah. That child, Isaac, was the father of Jacob/Israel, and the twelve sons of Israel were the ancestors of the twelve tribes according to the Bible. So Paul is in effect arguing that the true Israel has become the church—a doctrine that in later times was called "supersessionism" because it argued that Christians had superseded and replaced Jews in God's plan for salvation. Later, in Romans chapters 9–11, Paul seemingly draws back from this conclusion, though he does not explicitly renounce it. Rather, he seems to say that it is impossible to know what God will ultimately do about the salvation of the Jewish people, and in the meantime God has provided for the salvation of non-Jews by, in effect, grafting them onto Jewish stock. Down through the ages, however, Christians have assumed that Jews, as Jews, cannot be saved, and some Christians still believe that now.

In two places—John 8.44 and Revelation 2.9 (repeated in 3.9)—Jews are accused of being in the control of demonic powers. Jesus, in dialogue with Jewish followers who are withdrawing from him, says that their father is "the devil"; the author of Revelation similarly refers to "those who say they are Jews and are not, but are a synagogue of Satan." The specific reference in John's gospel seems to be only to those to whom Jesus is speaking—that is, those who, having once followed him, are now drawing back—but the influence of this verse has been pernicious. The Revelation passages are clearly aimed at those Jews who have not joined the Christian community, but who are arguing against and even persecuting it. They no doubt reflect the situation in the late first century or early second century, when the division between Judaism and Christianity was complete but both sides engaged in polemics and there were accusations and fears of apostasy. But to explain these passages is certainly not to condone them. The identification of Jews with Satan, along with the shameful treatment of Jews throughout Christian history as potential or actual traitors, apostates, betrayers, and murderers, still hinders Christian-Jewish relations in an interfaith and religiously complex world.

Finally, throughout John's gospel the opponents of Jesus are referred to as "the Jews." This term seems to refer primarily to Judaism's religious elite, what we might call the Temple party, plus those politically connected Jews who saw any potential insurrection as a threat to their status. Yet its use is so general and so widespread that in many places it makes the gospel read as if Jesus and his followers were something other than Jews—even though it is quite clear that Jesus observes Jewish religious practices and holidays, goes to the Temple, regards himself as a Jew when he is speaking to non-Jews, and so on. This use of the term "the Jews" to mean "opponents of Jesus" has caused much Christian hostility to Judaism even though the same gospel also contains Jesus' encounter with the Samaritan woman at the well, during which he says, "Salvation is from the Jews" (John 4.22).

Encountering the "Other" Today

All Christians are agreed at this point that slavery is wrong, and therefore the Bible is wrong to have tolerated it. Most Christians agree that the roles of women and the areas of life in which they function should be much wider than the Bible generally allows. Most Christians also agree that the New Testament view of Jews and Judaism is, at the least, flawed. But what should we do about these views now?

Defenses of the Bible usually follow one of two lines of argument: the chronological defense ("Everyone at the time thought slavery was acceptable") or the development defense ("Later texts are moving toward a more negative view of slavery, so all we've done is continue the trajectory"). But either of these approaches is ruinous for any other arguments that rely on the Bible's moral laws and try to apply them directly to our current situation.

The chronological defense—that the Bible simply reflects certain questionable mores of its time in areas where we have decided that we will not follow what the Bible says—leaves its proponents open to a damaging question: why not apply this selectivity to other areas? Why not argue that the Bible's sexual morality, particularly with regard to both heterosexual and gay and lesbian relationships, simply represents a worldview that we've outgrown?

Even worse is the trajectory approach. Take the issue of women's roles, for example. We read Paul's words in Galatians about how there is neither slave nor free, Jew nor Gentile, male nor female in Christ Jesus, a passage that many Christians quote with approval today. And then we read in the later letter of 1 Timothy (2.11–12), "Let a woman learn in silence with full submission. I permit no woman to teach or to have authority over a man; she is to keep silent." If there is a trajectory here, it is running in the wrong direction. There is certainly an effort on the part of the author of 1 Timothy to draw back from the equality and authority that women seem to have held in earlier Christian communities.

Clearly we need a different way of thinking about passages on topics such as these. In the case of those passages endorsing slavery, perhaps we can look at them in this way. The core meaning of being a slave is that one is completely dependent, at least economically, on another. That is why slavery can be used as a metaphor for one's relationship to God: it is a relationship of utter dependence. If we apply this to ourselves—and particularly if we keep in mind the Hebrew Bible's repetitions and reminders of how the Israelites were themselves slaves in Egypt—we can view it in two ways.

First, we can recognize that those who are dependent on us in economic terms, such as employees, have rights of their own as well as responsibilities to us. And we can recognize that we owe them obligations, that it is not just a matter of what they are doing for us but also of what we are doing for them.

The second thing we can keep in mind, particularly when we are dealing with those who are only intermittently or occasionally in a relationship of economic dependence to us— counter-clerks, waiters or waitresses, and so on—is that we and they share membership in the human race. For some of us, indeed, the words of the Bible could be paraphrased as, "Treat your waitress as you would wish to be treated. Remember that you were once a waitress yourself." For those who have never been forced to take a menial job, this may be a hard lesson to keep in mind, but it is vital that we all learn it. In our increasingly complex and interlocked world, we have to have clear rules by which we can operate with those who are "economically other" than we are.

When we look at the passages about women, what strikes me most clearly is how easily we can fall into generalizations about those who are "other" than we are. These passages are mostly written by men, addressed to men, and refer to women as a class rather than as individuals. As the story of Tamar reminds us, when we do allow an individual woman's experience to come before us, it can be shattering in its graphic portrayal of the pain of a human life. Women here, therefore, can stand in for all of those "strangers and aliens" whom we encounter in our daily lives— if it isn't women, or men, it is members of particular ethnic groups, religions, regions of the country or the world, professions—lawyers and politicians come in for a good deal of negative stereotyping—and so on. The solution, then, whenever we feel that we are being overtaken by the desire to stereotype and diminish, is to put before our minds one flesh-and-blood member of the group, about whom we are forced to have complex feelings. Nuance is the deadly enemy of simplistic ignorance.

The passages about Jews became of acute concern to Christians in the aftermath of World War II and the Holocaust of European Jewry. Most Christians are aware nowadays of the importance of guarding against the anti-Semitism that characterized much of Christian history. But in our world Jews can stand in for all of those who are "religiously other" than we are. At present, that would include Muslims. We have to resist with all our ability the hysteria that equates Islam with terrorism— to say nothing of the tendency to regard the players in the Middle East, primarily Jews and Islamic Arabs, as somehow essentially at opposite poles from each other. Those who support Israel— not so much Jews, who greatly vary in the degree to which they support the political actions of the state of Israel, but rather those Christians for whom the existence of Israel is a biblical mandate—tend to view Islam and the Arab states as implacable enemies and, at worst, as demonic. Those who want more justice for Palestinians, or who think our Middle Eastern policies are too slanted toward Israel, tend to demonize both Israeli and American Jews. Both these temptations have to be resisted because they can so easily become demonic in turn.

The "economically other," the "socially other," and the "religiously other" are often our deepest challenges. They bring before us in an acute form the mystery of creation in all of its diversity and incomprehensibility. And the Bible, no less than other aspects of human interaction with God, can simply reproduce the uncomprehending stance of a human being faced with a difference that he or she cannot fathom. In grappling with these biblical texts, we are really grappling with the challenges that life confronts us with nearly every day.

There are, as well, other categories of human beings with which we need to grapple. Those who are male, economically secure, heterosexual, and speaking to others within their own religious group can often read the Bible—which is largely addressed to those who are male, economically secure enough to be literate, heterosexual, and speaking to others of the same religious group—as endorsing all of our unthinking categorizations of "others." As we turn to a consideration of how to treat the "sexual other," as seen from the dominant heterosexual standpoint, all of the hard thinking that we have had to undertake with respect to slaves, women, and Jews will come into play. We are challenged to think about those who are different from us in new ways. And how we meet those challenges is a large part of how our characters grow, develop, and deepen—or conversely shrink, become shallow, and eventually dry up—in the course of our lives.

HOMOSEXUALITY

Is the Bible Straight about Gay People?

IN A TWO-PAGE advertisement in the *New York Times*, the American Society for the Defense of Tradition, Family and Property proposed a course of civil disobedience for Americans, particularly Roman Catholics, who were opposed to the institution of gay marriage.* The precipitating events were the decision by the California Supreme Court of May 15, 2008 that recognized gay marriage in that state, and the decision of Governor David Paterson of New York that all state agencies would recognize homosexual unions from other jurisdictions. The advertisement was careful to say that it was sympathetic to those who were born with a homosexual orientation, "who struggle with their weakness and strive to overcome it," and that the sponsors prayed for such people and also for "others who transform their sin into a reason for pride and *try to impose their lifestyle on society as a whole*" (emphasis added). But the organization went on to say, in the course of a lengthy and complex argument based on natural law, papal encyclicals, and various theologians, that "a Catholic who accepts the practice of homosexuality... as good renounces natural law principles confirmed by Divine Revelation and thus breaks the vow of fidelity made to Our Lord Jesus Christ at baptism." In other words, it is not possible to be Catholic while allowing the legitimacy of same-sex unions or homosexual intercourse, according to those (unnamed persons) who sponsored this advertisement. Nowhere does the advertisement allow for

the possibility of a homosexual person in a committed same-sex
relationship being a Christian; advocacy of the legitimacy of
homosexual marriage is presented, without evidence or argument, as the imposition of one's views on others. The fact that
confining marriage to heterosexuals is far more of an imposition is never acknowledged in the text of the advertisement.

On the very next day* the *Times* carried an account of the
funeral mass for the fashion designer Yves Saint Laurent, who
had died the previous Sunday, June 1. M. Saint Laurent's service
was held at the (Roman Catholic) St.-Roch Church in Paris,
where the French playwright Corneille is buried. The President
of France, numerous celebrities, and many admirers attended.
The coffin was draped in the French flag when it left the church
after the ceremony. Many of those in attendance received communion.

Among those attending was M. Saint Laurent's business and
life partner, Pierre Bergé, who spoke of their life together,
alluded to M. Saint Laurent's coming burial in Morocco at their
home, and said, "I never would have left you. Have we ever left
each other before? Even if I know that we will no longer share
a surge of emotion before a painting or a work of art. But I also
know that I will never forget what I owe you, and that one day
I will join you under the Moroccan palms." M. Saint Laurent
and M. Bergé had entered into a civil union before the designer's
death.

Like other organizations in today's world, the Roman
Catholic Church is trying to balance its traditional teachings
with new attitudes and increased knowledge about the realities
of human nature, including sexual orientation. Officially, the
Roman Catholic Church does not recognize the legitimacy of
homosexual intercourse, and regards it as a sign of a disordered
nature. Officially also, the church is opposed to legal efforts on
behalf of civil rights for gay and lesbian persons. Nevertheless, at
least one parish church in Paris managed to find room for a gay
couple—albeit a very prominent gay couple—to have a funeral
mass, presided over by a priest, when one partner died.

---

* June 6, 2008, A7.

Our society increasingly accepts persons who are openly homosexual in a variety of positions—in Congress and state and local legislatures, in courts of law, as teachers, as athletes, as performers and actors. Straight movie actors play gay roles; gay movie actors play straight roles. Social invitations include spouses, partners, or significant others. Wedding announcement pages in newspapers often include the commitment ceremonies of same-sex partners; battered wife laws are extended to apply to battered partners. Employment and housing are increasingly nondiscriminatory with regard to sexual orientation, while workplace rules apply to both gay and straight behavior—for instance, in cases of relationships between supervisor and subordinate. This is as it should be. A gay boss hitting on a gay employee should be no more, and no less, liable to discipline than is a straight boss hitting on a straight employee. A lesbian professor exploiting her power over a lesbian student is engaging in conduct that is just as wrong as would be a heterosexual professor extorting sexual favors from a heterosexual student—no more, no less. A brutalizing sexual relationship between gay or lesbian partners should be subject to legal intervention, as is an abusive relationship between straight partners.

This increasing acceptance, however—at least in some areas of the country and among some groups—has, perhaps predictably, brought about a reaction. Some people fear that even condoning or tolerating the rights of gay couples will undermine traditional marriages. (It is not clear how this will happen, but many people make the argument nonetheless.) Accordingly, "gay civil rights" movements have prompted counter-measures—amendments banning gay marriage, for example. Some African-American leaders have objected to analogies between racial civil rights and rights for gay people, and between the historic and ongoing racial civil rights movement and gay activism (though many African Americans support full rights for gay and lesbian persons).

In the religious sphere, this battle has been concentrated in two areas over which Christians are sharply divided. The first has to do with whether it is licit to ordain gays and lesbians, especially those in committed relationships, to positions of religious leadership. The second is whether individual church bodies should bless or otherwise preside over ceremonies of commitment between same-sex couples. In some denominations, efforts either to undertake one or both of these actions, or to thwart them, have led to ruptures of varying degrees of seriousness. The United Presbyterian Church has had a long struggle with some of its conservative members over whether the Reverend Jane Spahr, a Presbyterian minister in California, has contravened the church's *Book of Order* (its equivalent of canon law) by presiding over unions of same-sex couples. The United Methodist Church has continued to reject calls for changing its stance that the practice of homosexuality is "incompatible with Christian teaching," but the margins of the vote to uphold the language keep shrinking.*

Before we look at the biblical passages dealing with homosexuality in the broadest sense, we will have to make clearer what it is we are talking about when we discuss homosexuality itself, "gay marriage," and other issues.

Clarifying the Issues
Marriage in our society has two aspects, one religious and one legal or civil. The religious one is a matter that various denominations, Christian and non-Christian, define in their own ways. For some Christian traditions, marriage is sacramental—that is, it is a conveyer of divine grace—but for others this is not the case. The religious significance of marriage, therefore, is a matter for each religious body to decide in its own way. And people are free to accept or reject a particular religious view of marriage, or any religious view at all.

Legally, marriage is a contract that two people enter into before the presence of witnesses. It is legally binding in various ways, and brings with it responsibilities and benefits. As a matter of civil rights, the argument over "gay marriage" basically means that if two people of the same sex wish to make a commitment to each other, they should be bound by the same social responsibilities that bind opposite-sex partners and share in the same benefits: inheritance and insurance rights, for instance. Many

---

* "Presbyterian high court clears pastor of censure for same-sex weddings" and "Methodists retain policies on homosexuality," *The Christian Century* (June 3, 2008), 14–16.

employers now—to take just one example—extend health insurance coverage to domestic partners as well as to spouses in a legally defined relationship, and same-sex marriage is simply a way of recognizing and affirming in civil law the reality of many peoples' lives.

Marriage as a religious or sacramental rite is far different. In our society the two are confused because the actual performance of the contractual agreement *can* be witnessed by a religious official—priest, minister, rabbi, or imam. Although desirable in some ways, this practice conflates the *legal* marriage—the contractual arrangement, in which civil society takes an interest—with the *religious* rite, which is of concern only to the members of the particular religious group to which the couple and the presiding minister belong. Matters would be much clearer, however, if we simply regarded obtaining the marriage license—issued by the civil power—as the legal contract. Then the witnessing ceremony—whether conducted by a civil authority, like a mayor or judge, or a religious one—is simply the necessary *legal* procedure that means the couple have publicly entered into the contract. If people wish to add religious sanction to their contractual obligations—prohibiting the possibility of divorce, for example—that is their right, but the state has nothing to say about it one way or the other.

There is no legal way of forcing any given religious group to recognize same-sex partnerships even if civil marriage becomes available throughout the entire country. Just as with the ordination of women, where no court would enforce equal opportunity law against a denomination that did not ordain women by requiring it to do so, so with same-sex marriage. No court would enforce civil marriage laws by requiring a religious group to accept same-sex marriage if that group held that it could not validly marry same-sex partners. Much of the hysteria about this issue, therefore, ignores the actual legal situation.

Another set of issues that we must clarify has to do with what we mean by the word "homosexual." This involves, it seems to me, making at least three distinctions.

First, we must recognize that for some people, sexual arousal primarily occurs with members of their own sex. It does not matter, for the purposes of discovering what the Bible has to say about this topic, whether this is the result of genetic predisposition, life experiences, or some combination of the two. The only thing that matters is that we recognize the phenomenon, and accept the testimony of those for whom this is the case that it is not something they "choose" but is rather simply the way they are. This should not be difficult for heterosexuals to imagine, since for them, sexual arousal occurs only or mainly with the opposite sex. All they need to do is switch the genders to understand the reality. Asking a gay person to marry a member of the opposite sex—though this occurs, often as the result of social pressure—is as oppressive as it would be to ask a straight person to marry a member of the same sex.

There are a couple of subsidiary matters that we need to be clear about with this first point. The first is that although some people are sexually attracted to members of the same sex, they do not need to act on this attraction. Gays and lesbians can choose not to engage in sexual activity just as straight people can. Or they can choose to engage in sexual activity with only one other person despite the attractiveness of other people—just as straight people can.

The second distinction is that we are focusing on sexual attraction between mature human beings, whether heterosexual or homosexual, and not the sexual attraction of an adult for a sexually immature child or a young teenager. In some people's minds, homosexuality is equated with pederasty or pedophilia (sexual attraction to pre-pubescent children) or ephebephilia (sexual attraction to post-pubescent but still young teenagers), but this is not a legitimate association. Some heterosexuals are also pedophiles or ephebephiles, and little girls are as much at risk as little boys, perhaps more so, for sexual molestation.

This matter is important because people who are outspoken on the evils of homosexuality sometimes invoke pedophilia in order to confuse this issue. They will say, "If we legalize homosexual relationships, what is to keep us from legalizing sexual relationships between adults and children?" The answer is that we don't—because children cannot validly consent to a sexual relationship. Those people who are *only* sexually attracted to children have to be prevented from carrying out their desires because it is the responsibility of the wider adult culture to protect children from such experiences. There is no analogy to be drawn between a sexual relationship involving two mature adults who have freely entered into it and any relationship involving an adult and a child, because by definition the child cannot have made a mature choice. Some children or young teenagers, having been forced into a sexual relationship with an adult, later act toward other adults in a sexually provocative, aggressive, or seductive manner, but these children have been illegitimately introduced to such behavior by the first adult—or, even worse, group of adults—who sexually exploited them. Other adults who come into contact with these unfortunate victims are responsible for resisting their seductiveness because the adult should take the responsible role.

The second major distinction we must make is between persons who are sexually aroused only by members of their own sex and those who engage in homosexual activity because of their situation. This is more common than we generally acknowledge: same-sex environments, such as prisons, some private schools, military units (particularly in the past, as with ocean-going sailing ships), and religious orders, can give rise to homosexual encounters between people who are entirely or primarily heterosexual. Prison rape (that is, the rape of one prisoner by another, not the rape of prisoners by guards), though the vast majority of cases are obviously male-on-male, is committed almost entirely by heterosexuals. They choose same-sex partners not because they are suddenly "converted" to homosexuality, but because such partners are the only ones available.

This kind of sexual activity should alert us to another aspect of sexual arousal: it is not only an attractive person who can be sexually arousing. A weaker person can also arouse someone stronger, and therefore a power differential between two sexual partners can itself be the cause of sexual arousal. This reality may lie behind some of the sexual-abuse scandal in the Roman Catholic Church: some of the adults who abused small boys may not have been homosexual at all, but may have been taking sexual advantage of the available victims, who were young male altar boys. Nor may the adult's arousal be due to the specific gender of the victim; as with sexual relations between same-sex prisoners, the essential factor may be the power differential between the perpetrator and the victim. The connection between power and sexual arousal may be a key fact in understanding what homosexual relationships actually meant to the writers of the New Testament.

The third major distinction, as I have said already, is between gays and lesbians who are sexually active, and those who choose not to have a sexual relationship. Just as there are straight people who never have a sexual relationship with a member of the opposite sex—either vowed celibates, like members of religious orders, or single people who for whatever reason have never had a sexual partner—so there are homosexual persons who are celibate by choice or necessity. Simply because this is possible, however, does not justify making it mandatory. Mandatory celibacy is not a spiritual discipline—it is a penalty. And outside of protecting children from sexual exploitation, there is no justification for imposing a penalty on something that a person has not freely chosen.

This extensive discussion is the essential background when we turn to consider the biblical texts having to do with homosexuality in one way or another. There are actually very few of them—if we stretch the theme of homosexuality to the utmost, we can come up with eight or so passages, not more. We will look at each of them and try to determine, first, what they might mean, and second, how we might apply them to our lives—if we can apply them at all. Some may have very little relevance; others may be dealing with homosexuality in a way that we can no longer accept. We will have to look at each text as it stands, and as it fits into the larger biblical framework, before we will know the answer.

Sodom and Gomorrah

The first text, from chapter 19 of the Book of Genesis, is that concerning the destruction of Sodom and Gomorrah. Most often this narrative is truncated in a misleading way. We will look at the chapter in its entirety, to see what moral lessons we might draw from it.

> The two angels came to Sodom in the evening, and Lot was sitting in the gateway of Sodom. When Lot saw them, he rose to meet them, and bowed down with his face to the ground. He said, "Please, my lords, turn aside to your servant's house and spend the night, and wash your feet; then you can rise early and go on your way." They said, "No; we will spend the night in the square." But he urged them strongly; so they turned aside to him and entered his house; and he made them a feast, and baked unleavened bread, and they ate. But before they lay down, the men of the city, the men of Sodom, both young and old, all the people to the last man, surrounded the house; and they called to Lot, "Where are the men who came to you tonight? Bring them out to us, so that we may know them." Lot went out of the door to the men, shut the door after him, and said, "I beg you, my brothers, do not act so wickedly. Look, I have two daughters who have not known a man; let me bring them out to you, and do to them as you please; only do nothing to these men, for they have come under the shelter of my roof." But they replied, "Stand back!" And they said, "This fellow came here as an alien, and he would play the judge! Now we will deal worse with you than with them." Then they pressed hard against the man Lot, and came near the door to break it down. But the men inside reached out their hands and brought Lot into the house with them, and shut the door. And they struck with blindness the men who were at the door of the house, both small and great, so that they were unable to find the door.
>
> Then the men said to Lot, "Have you anyone else here? Sons-in-law, sons, daughters, or anyone you have in the city— bring them out of the place. For we are about to destroy this

place, because the outcry against its people has become great
before the LORD, and the LORD has sent us to destroy it." So
Lot went out and said to his sons-in-law, who were to marry
his daughters, "Up, get out of this place; for the LORD is about
to destroy the city." But he seemed to his sons-in-law to be
jesting.

When morning dawned, the angels urged Lot, saying,
"Get up, take your wife and your two daughters who are here,
or else you will be consumed in the punishment of the city."
But he lingered; so the men seized him and his wife and his
two daughters by the hand, the LORD being merciful to him,
and they brought him out and left him outside the city. When
they had brought them outside, they said, "Flee for your life;
do not look back or stop anywhere in the Plain; flee to the
hills, or else you will be consumed." And Lot said to them,
"Oh, no, my lords; your servant has found favor with you, and
you have shown me great kindness in saving my life; but I
cannot flee to the hills, for fear the disaster will overtake me
and I die. Look, that city is near enough to flee to, and it is a
little one. Let me escape there—is it not a little one?—and my
life will be saved!" He said to him, "Very well, I grant you this
favor too, and will not overthrow the city of which you have
spoken. Hurry, escape there, for I can do nothing until you
arrive there." Therefore the city was called Zoar [i.e., "little"].
The sun had risen on the earth when Lot came to Zoar.

Then the LORD rained on Sodom and Gomorrah sulfur
and fire from the LORD out of heaven; and he overthrew
those cities, and all the Plain, and all the inhabitants of the
cities, and what grew on the ground. But Lot's wife, behind
him, looked back, and she became a pillar of salt.

Abraham went early in the morning to the place where
he had stood before the LORD; and he looked down toward
Sodom and Gomorrah and toward all the land of the Plain
and saw the smoke of the land going up like the smoke of a
furnace.

So it was that, when God destroyed the cities of the Plain,
God remembered Abraham, and sent Lot out of the midst of

the overthrow, when he overthrew the cities in which Lot had settled.

Now Lot went up out of Zoar and settled in the hills with his two daughters, for he was afraid to stay in Zoar; so he lived in a cave with his two daughters. And the firstborn said to the younger, "Our father is old, and there is not a man on earth to come in to us after the manner of all the world. Come, let us make our father drink wine, and we will lie with him, so that we may preserve offspring through our father." So they made their father drink wine that night; and the firstborn went in, and lay with her father; he did not know when she lay down or when she rose. On the next day, the firstborn said to the younger, "Look, I lay last night with my father; let us make him drink wine tonight also; then you go in and lie with him, so that we may preserve offspring through our father." So they made their father drink wine that night also; and the younger rose, and lay with him; and he did not know when she lay down or when she rose. Thus both the daughters of Lot became pregnant by their father. The firstborn bore a son, and named him Moab; he is the ancestor of the Moabites to this day. The younger also bore a son and named him Ben-ammi; he is the ancestor of the Ammonites to this day. (Genesis 19.1–38)

To read this story through is to see, first of all, how difficult it is to draw any kind of positive moral lessons from it. Let us look at the story by beginning at the end. The daughters of Lot conceive the ancestors of two of Israel's neighboring peoples in an act of drunken incest. The story does not condemn this action (though there may be some impetus to demean the ancestry of these neighboring tribes by telling a story of their shameful beginnings). The Moabites, in particular, were close to Israel and a woman of Moab, Ruth, was one of the ancestors of King David. So, if anything, this story might be slightly slanted in favor of what Lot's daughters did.

The escape of Lot and his family from Sodom is due to two things: Lot's relation to Abraham (Genesis 11.27; he was Abraham's nephew), and God's graciousness to Lot. It is not clear why, other than the relation to Abraham, Lot deserved this grace, since he is willing to offer his virgin daughters for a gang rape in order to protect his guests. In addition, Lot's wife seems to be very badly treated: though she does disobey the command not to look back—and surely, looking back would be a natural reaction to a scene of unparalleled destruction—she is punished just as much as are the inhabitants of Sodom, since (presumably) being turned into a pillar of salt is fatal.

Finally, there is the issue for which this story has become famous (or infamous), and which has given the name of "sodomy" to homosexual intercourse: the attempted homosexual rape of Lot's guests by the inhabitants of Sodom. We should note that the crowd outside Lot's house specifically cites the fact that Lot is an *alien* as part of their motivation. Though Lot himself is not threatened with rape, the men clearly express disdain for his presumption in trying to tell them what to do.

In fact, the threatened rape of the guests is far more likely to be a way of asserting the power of the residents of Sodom over "outsiders" than it is to be an expression of homosexual lust. In that culture, to subject another male to rape—to force him to be sexually submissive, as women were supposed to be—is a way of asserting or maintaining dominance over him. Those outside the dominant group in a particular area are therefore at risk of being demeaned by being forced to adopt the woman's position in sexual intercourse. That is the "shameful" position in which the men of Sodom wish to place Lot's guests, and that is the action against which Lot protests—and which he is willing to avert by offering his daughters as objects of sexual predation. The men reject the offer of the daughters, then, not because they are homosexuals—that is, not because they are not sexually attracted to women—but because their proposed rape is not on account of sexual attraction, but on account of the wish to express power over the alien, including power over the resident alien, Lot, by disregarding his efforts to prevent their action.

In a similar incident, recounted in Judges 19.1–30, the men wishing to rape a male stranger in their town are prevented but are given the man's concubine, whom they rape in his stead. A Levite and his concubine have been sheltered by an old man who is resident in the city of Gibeah. They eat together, and when night has fallen,

> the men of the city, a perverse lot [*bene-beli'al, literally* "sons of worthlessness," not a comment on sexual proclivities], surrounded the house, and started pounding on the door. They said to the old man, the master of the house, "Bring out the man who came into your house, so that we may have intercourse with him." And the man, the master of the house, went out to them and said to them, "No, my brothers, do not act so wickedly. Since this man is my guest, do not do this vile thing. Here are my virgin daughter and his concubine; let me bring them out now. Ravish them and do whatever you want to them; but against this man do not do such a vile thing." But the men would not listen to him. So the man seized his concubine, and put her out to them. They wantonly raped her, and abused her all through the night until the morning. And as the dawn began to break, they let her go. (19.22–25)

This narrative shows clearly that the motivating force behind these attempted rapes is the desire to subjugate or humiliate the stranger. The concubine is acceptable because she is the man's property, though she is not as good for the purposes of humiliation as the man himself would be. But the fact that the men of the city carry out their sexual subjugation on a woman indicates that homosexual orientation is not the issue here.

We can therefore derive two lessons from the tale of Lot's residence in Sodom, but neither of them has to do with the condemnation of consensual homosexual relationships. The first is that any nationalistic or group pride on our part should be suppressed in the recognition that all groups have shadowy origins, and no one is descended from ancestors with absolutely clean hands (or histories). To be sure, not all clans or ethnic groups have drunken incest in their backgrounds, but we all know (or suspect) that if the full truth came out, no group would have arisen from honorable roots. We can honor our own ethnic groups or nations for the good they have done, but any effort to develop an intrinsic worth for them is doomed.

The second lesson we can take away from this passage is particularly striking in light of the position of the United States in the international political community. These Scripture texts make clear that God does not approve of the sexual humiliation of foreigners—be they "aliens," Levites, or Iraqis. Therefore the actions of the U.S. soldiers who have sexually humiliated Arab prisoners should have been condemned outright by every Christian in the country. The current administration and the Congress should have been assiduous in rooting out the tendencies toward this abuse of prisoners no matter how high in the command structure or the civilian administration they reached.

The Holiness Code

Other Old Testament texts that appear to deal unequivocally with the question of homosexual behavior are found in the Book of Leviticus, from the Holiness Code:

> You shall not give any of your offspring to sacrifice them to Molech, and so profane the name of your God: I am the LORD. You shall not lie with a male as with a woman; it is an abomination. (Leviticus 18.21–22)

> The LORD spoke to Moses, saying: Say further to the people of Israel: Any of the people of Israel, or of the aliens who reside in Israel, who give any of their offspring to Molech shall be put to death; the people of the land shall stone them to death. I myself will set my face against them, and will cut them off from the people, because they have given of their offspring to Molech, defiling my sanctuary and profaning my holy name. And if the people of the land should ever close their eyes to them, when they give of their offspring to Molech, and do not put them to death, I myself will set my face against them and against their family, and will cut them off from among their people, them and all who follow them in prostituting themselves to Molech.

If any turn to mediums and wizards, prostituting
themselves to them, I will set my face against them, and will
cut them off from the people. Consecrate yourselves therefore,
and be holy; for I am the LORD your God. Keep my statutes,
and observe them; I am the LORD; I sanctify you. All who
curse father or mother shall be put to death; having cursed
father or mother, their blood is upon them.

If a man commits adultery with the wife of his neighbor,
both the adulterer and the adulteress shall be put to death.
The man who lies with his father's wife has uncovered his
father's nakedness; both of them shall be put to death; their
blood is upon them. If a man lies with his daughter-in-law,
both of them shall be put to death; they have committed
perversion [*tebel, literally* "confusion, mingling"], their blood is
upon them. If a man lies with a male as with a woman, both
of them have committed an abomination; they shall be put to
death; their blood is upon them. (Leviticus 20.1–13)

These verses condemning sexual intercourse between two
men seem unambiguous, until we consider two things. The first
is the context in which each of the verses is propounded: they
are both preceded by prohibitions of worshiping Molech.
Though the actual identification of the biblical name Molech
with any ancient Near Eastern god is unclear, the biblical view
of this deity is that it required child sacrifice (2 Kings 23.10) and
possibly, in this passage, witchcraft and divination. One theory
about the name Molech is that it combines the Hebrew conso-
nants for "king" (*melekh—m-l-kh*) with the vowels for "shame"
(*bosheth—o-e*). The god's name in Hebrew would thus suggest
"shameful king."

In any case, in the second Leviticus passage the condemnation of intercourse between two males is immediately preceded
by a condemnation of "mingling," a serious transgression, the
crossing of a boundary between things that should be kept separate. Such a prohibition of "mingling" is a part of the biblical
idea of purity, the most serious transgression of which is the
crossing of the boundary between life and death. Witchcraft and

divination sometimes involve efforts to communicate with the dead (as in King Saul's visit to the witch, or medium, at Endor, during which he summons the ghost of the prophet Samuel from Sheol, 1 Samuel 28.6–19).

The prohibition against intercourse between two males, therefore—like that between a son and a stepmother, two people closely related by marriage—may be intended to safeguard the integrity of various sexual pairings as part of a larger ideal of fully integral being: no mingled fabrics, no cross-species interbreeding, no fields sown with two different kinds of seed, and so on (Leviticus 19.19). Proper boundaries must be maintained, or such mixtures will threaten to weaken the fabric of social relationships. Later, marriages between Israelite people (or Jews) and others are forbidden, and those in existing intermarriages are forced to dissolve them (Ezra 9.1–15). Since gay and lesbian people are full human beings with their own integrity—and since any effort to force a homosexual person into a heterosexual marriage undermines rather than promotes integrity of life—these strictures against mingling would lead us to take the opposite view: homosexual relationships can be expressions of personal integration, not the reverse.

The second thing to consider is the way in which the word translated "abomination" is used elsewhere in the Bible. This word, to 'evah, does not have a very precise meaning, at least one that is known today: it connotes "something abhorrent," to be avoided. It occurs over a hundred times in the Hebrew text, and in nearly every occurrence, outside these verses in Leviticus, it is generally applied to an unacceptable religious practice or an unjust economic or social action. In Deuteronomy 17.1, for instance, it is an abomination to sacrifice an ox or a sheep that is defective (in other words, to try to cheat God by offering something that is of lesser value to you). In Deuteronomy 25.13–16, a different form of fraudulent behavior is prohibited: it is an abomination to cheat your customers with dishonest weights and measures.

The Book of Ezekiel is particularly suggestive with regard to this word. In Ezekiel's prophetic denunciations generally, idolatry is symbolized by sexual immorality of a heterosexual kind: Israel is condemned as an adulterous woman, a prostitute, and often in extravagant language (16.35–43). The word to 'evah occurs repeatedly (16.43, 47, 50). In verses 46 and following, Ezekiel compares the sins of Israel to those of Samaria to the north and Sodom to the south. Here, if anywhere, we could expect the use of homosexual imagery to condemn idolatry, given the later (nonbiblical) association of Sodom with such imagery. But here is what Ezekiel actually says about Sodom:

> This was the guilt of your sister Sodom: she and her daughters had pride, excess of food, and prosperous ease, but did not aid the poor and needy. (16.49)

Apparently, sodomy is a more appropriate term as the name for economic injustice than it is as the name for homosexual practice.

One other place in which this word "abomination" or "abhorrent thing" occurs is of interest as well. In Deuteronomy we read:

> A woman shall not wear a man's apparel, nor shall a man put on a woman's garment; for whoever does such things is abhorrent to the LORD your God. (22.5)

The literal rendering of this would be, "a woman shall not put on anything of a man, and a man shall not wear a woman's outer garment." The NRSV here translates the words as they are generally understood. This verse prohibits wearing clothing (or, perhaps, adornment) that is associated with members of the opposite sex. The law gives no reason for this, but it seems to be another example of the prohibitions of "mingling" that we have seen elsewhere. Slightly later in the same chapter (vv. 9–11), there are the familiar prohibitions against sowing with two kinds of seed, plowing with an ox and donkey yoked together, or wearing clothing made of two different kinds of fabric. We are not meant to suppose that cross-dressing is necessarily associated in the Bible with homosexuality; the context of the verse gives no indication that this is the case, and the occurrence of the same word for "abomination" is not enough, as its use in other contexts should make clear. Furthermore, in our culture, while some homosexual men do wear women's clothing or adornment on occasion, heterosexual men do as well, and most homosexuals do not engage in cross-dressing.

Historically, after the Reformation, various Protestant groups regarded this verse as binding on Christians, and Puritans therefore were opposed to the theater (including the plays of Christopher Marlowe, William Shakespeare, Ben Johnson, and other classics of English literature) because the performances used young men (before their voices changed) in women's roles. This naturally required the male actors to dress in women's clothes; it was regarded, at the time, as immodest for women to act or appear onstage in a public performance of such a sort (private theatricals in houses of the nobility were a different matter).

At the present time, however, our current Western culture largely ignores this command. Women wear slacks, men's shirts, neckties, and other articles of clothing associated with males, both to work and for more casual occasions, and very few people seem to be bothered by this, or raise any objection. Men generally do not, in the same way, wear dresses or skirts in ordinary circumstances, but men do wear women's clothing. During the 2008 race for the Republican nomination for president, for example, pictures of former mayor Rudolph Giuliani in elaborate gowns, wearing makeup, jewelry, and a wig, circulated widely. Mr. Giuliani had appeared at several public events, including charitable fundraisers, dressed as a woman for comic purposes. Yet there were no prominent calls for him not to pursue the nomination, in spite of the existence of pictures of the former mayor committing an abomination, according to the text of Deuteronomy—the same word that is used to characterize homosexual intercourse.

When we have fully considered these texts—Genesis 19, Leviticus 18 and 20, and Judges 19—we have examined all of the places in the Hebrew Bible that deal with homosexuality. We should note that only two of these places are actual prohibitions; the other two, in Genesis and Judges, are narratives in which proposed homosexual rape is condemned for reasons that are not stated.

It is also interesting to note—although it is not possible to draw a firm conclusion from a negative phenomenon—that Deuteronomy, which is a later legal compilation than Leviticus, contains no condemnation of homosexual intercourse (Deuteronomy probably dates from the seventh century and Leviticus, though it was likely assembled in its final form during the sixth-century exile, is comprised largely of materials dating back as far as the tenth century BCE). This may indicate that the particular identification of idolatry with such behavior had disappeared by the time Deuteronomy was compiled, since it repeats many other laws that appear in Exodus, Leviticus, and Numbers. The association of Sodom with economic injustice in Ezekiel in the sixth century, especially given Ezekiel's clear concern with idolatry in general, and his use of sexual imagery (adultery) to denounce it, would seem to reinforce the point that condemnations of homosexuality receded or vanished in the later period of Israel's existence.

The New Testament

What about the New Testament? Despite the vehemence with which some of us invoke "biblical values" in speaking out against homosexuality, nowhere in the gospels, and particularly nowhere in the words of Jesus, is there any condemnation of homosexuality. In fact, Jesus is relatively uninterested in sexual sin: he mentions "fornication" (Matthew 15.19, Mark 7.21—essentially one occurrence, since they are parallel accounts), and he condemns adultery, but his main emphasis is clearly elsewhere. We must look outside the gospels for any New Testament treatment of this topic. There are four places that may deal in any significant way with homosexuality.

The letter of Jude, one of the shortest in the New Testament, contains the following passage:

> Now I desire to remind you, though you are fully informed,
> that the Lord, who once for all saved a people out of the land

of Egypt, afterward destroyed those who did not believe. And
the angels who did not keep their own position, but left their
proper dwelling, he has kept in eternal chains in deepest
darkness for the judgment of the great day. Likewise, Sodom
and Gomorrah and the surrounding cities, which, in the same
manner as they, *ekporneusasai* ["engaged in *porneia, fornication"]
and pursued *sarkos heteras* ["other flesh"], serve as an example
by undergoing a punishment of eternal fire. (vv. 5–7)

This is a remarkably unclear passage, and it is therefore difficult
and dangerous to build any great moral edifice on it. What the
author of the letter seems to be saying, however, is that God will
punish those who have abandoned belief in Jesus as Lord (verse
4) and will judge them as severely as God judged the angels who
came down and had intercourse with human women (Genesis
6.1–4) and those inhabitants of Sodom who wished to have
intercourse with the angelic visitors of Lot (Genesis 19). In other
words, the condemnation here seems to be of those who want
to have intercourse with angels, not those who want to have
same-sex relations. And given the general biblical metaphor of
sexual intercourse and adultery as standing for religious unfaithfulness and idolatry—and especially given the condemnation
here of illicit relations between human beings and angels—it is
more plausible that the passage is primarily condemning
unhealthy spiritual exploration. The desire to have intercourse
with angels, or any effort to associate with the kinds of angels
who want to have intercourse with human beings, would thus
stand for efforts to have the kinds of religious experiences that
lead to idolatry, denial of the lordship of Jesus Christ, and general unfaithfulness.*

This theme of idolatry and false teaching associated with sexual immorality also appears in two other New Testament letters
that possibly mention homosexual practice. In 1 Corinthians,
Paul writes:

Do you not know that wrongdoers will not inherit the
kingdom of God? Do not be deceived! Fornicators, idolaters,
adulterers, male prostitutes [*malakoi*], sodomites [*arsenokoitai*],

---

* 2 Peter 2.4–16 repeats the text of Jude, but there is nothing in the epistle
that differentiates its treatment of sexual sins from that in Jude—essentially,
they are the same.

thieves, the greedy, drunkards, revilers, robbers—none of these will inherit the kingdom of God. (6.9–10)

And in 1 Timothy, the writer—after warning against other doctrines, myths, speculations, meaningless talk, a lack of understanding of spiritual things, and other tendencies that might undermine true faith (1.3–7)—goes on to say:

> Now we know that the law is good, if one uses it legitimately. This means understanding that the law is laid down not for the innocent but for the lawless and disobedient, for the godless and sinful, for the unholy and profane, for those who kill their father or mother, for murderers, fornicators, sodomites [*arsenokoitais*], slave traders [or "kidnappers"; *literally* "stealers of men"], liars, perjurers, and whatever else is contrary to the sound teaching that conforms to the glorious gospel of the blessed God, which he entrusted to me. (1.8–11)

Before we deal with the precise meaning of these words, note once again the general context: it is idolatry, following false teachings, and general flouting of the law that are condemned in these passages. We will look more closely at this association with idolatry, and what it might mean, when we deal with the one other New Testament passage having to do with homosexuality, and the most extensive one in the entire Bible: the first chapter of Paul's letter to the Romans.

The two words possibly having to do with sexual behavior in use here—*malakos* and *arsenokoites*—are difficult to translate. (The translation for *arsenokoites* used in the NRSV, "sodomite," is not a good choice because it does not represent anything that is in the Greek text, it brings in an unsupported allusion to the story of Sodom, and, since "sodomites" is never used in the Bible itself, even to refer to "residents of Sodom," it perpetuates an unbiblical word.)

Malakos means "soft" and, in contexts such as the one here, generally connotes effeminacy. In other words, it is as much a sneer as a technical term. "Limp-wristed" might be a contemporary rendition. If it refers to behavior at all—and that is

unclear—it would mean a man who submits to sexual intercourse. If, however, it simply means "the effeminate" (as the King
James, Rheims, and New American Standard Bible translations
render it), then the difficulty is this: the passage is condemning
someone for a characteristic and not an action—for *being* homosexual, in effect. Given what we now know about homosexual
orientation, this would be a very faulty moral vision.

In fact, in the Roman world this may indicate an analogous
situation to that which we examined in the context of the
accounts of Lot in Sodom and the Levite and his concubine in
Judges: homosexual rape as a way of demeaning aliens and
strangers. Of the two types of homosexual relations in classical
culture, that between an older man and a younger one (a sort of
initiatory experience that is alluded to in Plato's *Symposium*) and
that between a superior and inferior (for instance a master and
a slave), *malakos* may be the term that indicates the latter sort of
relationship is under discussion. In that case, the shamefulness of
being a *malakos* is caused by the demeaning fact (to classical
thinkers) of being put in the woman's position in sexual intercourse—that is, of being the one who is penetrated rather than
being the penetrator. A male who accepts this position, or who
is forced into it, is thereby humiliated or shamed.

Some, at least, of the energy of condemnation of homosexual intercourse in the New Testament may therefore be due to
the view, then prevalent in the wider society, that to take a
woman's position in the sexual act is by its very nature to lower
oneself to a woman's status. If that is the case, we would need to
think very carefully about whether we want to carry forward
this view of homosexuality, since it is confused with ideas about
women's status and the meaning of sexual positions that we no
longer agree with. It may even be the case that the New Testament writers have taken over these assumptions too uncritically
from their own milieu.

Arsenokoites is even more difficult. It is unusual, a compound
combining words meaning "male" (*arsen*) and "bed" (*koite*), leading to the assumption that it means "[a male taking] a male to
bed [for sexual intercourse]." The phrases I have supplied within

brackets represent what has to be supplied before the word can be associated with homosexuality. Those who have studied its usage elsewhere say that, contextually, it seems to mean something more like "those who exploit someone sexually"—a meaning that would fit its association with "thieves" in the Corinthians passage and with "slave traders" or "kidnappers" in 1 Timothy. Applying this term to people who exploit others sexually—by pimping, forced prostitution, selling people into sexual slavery, and so on—might be a better way to understand this word, and a better way of looking at the passages dealing with this kind of sexual immorality, than viewing them as condemning a consensual, nonexploitative homosexual relationship between mature adults.

This leaves only Paul's letter to the Romans, which contains the most extensive passage in the New Testament that deals with this topic—and the only one in the Bible that possibly mentions sexual relationships between women:

> For the wrath of God is revealed from heaven against all ungodliness and wickedness of those who by their wickedness suppress the truth. For what can be known about God is plain to them, because God has shown it to them. Ever since the creation of the world his eternal power and divine nature, invisible though they are, have been understood and seen through the things he has made. So they are without excuse; for though they knew God, they did not honor him as God or give thanks to him, but they became futile in their thinking, and their senseless minds were darkened. Claiming to be wise, they became fools; and they exchanged the glory of the immortal God for images resembling a mortal human being or birds or four-footed animals or reptiles.
>
> Therefore God gave them up in the lusts of their hearts to impurity, to the degrading of their bodies among themselves, because they exchanged the truth about God for a lie and worshiped and served the creature rather than the Creator, who is blessed forever! Amen.

> For this reason God gave them up to degrading passions.
> Their women exchanged natural intercourse for unnatural,
> and in the same way also the men, giving up natural
> intercourse with women, were consumed with passion for
> one another. Men committed shameless acts with men and
> received in their own persons the due penalty for their error.
> And since they did not see fit to acknowledge God, God
> gave them up to a debased mind and to things that should not
> be done. They were filled with every kind of wickedness, evil,
> covetousness, malice. Full of envy, murder, strife, deceit,
> craftiness, they are gossips, slanderers, God-haters, insolent,
> haughty, boastful, inventors of evil, rebellious toward parents,
> foolish, faithless, heartless, ruthless. They know God's decree,
> that those who practice such things deserve to die—yet they
> not only do them but even applaud others who practice
> them. (1.18–32)

As with much of Paul's writing, this passage is very densely
woven and not very well laid out logically. Furthermore, it makes
some assumptions that, although they were perfectly clear in the
world in which Paul was writing, we have to spell out for ourselves in order to make Paul's meaning clearer. Therefore I will
begin by trying to paraphrase part of the argument in order to
clarify the point that Paul is making.

> Everyone accepts the fact that the world as we see it in front
> of us didn't just come into being—it was created, and in fact
> it was created by God. To ignore this, or to try to pretend that
> it isn't the case, is to try to make yourself stupid. And when
> you try to make yourself stupid, you very often succeed! You
> muddy your own thought—you make your mind a place of
> darkness rather than light. That's the penalty for trying to
> ignore something that's staring you in the face.
>
> So what happens, then, when you try to pretend that
> something isn't so? You start living a lie in all the rest of your
> life, as well. You can't divorce your knowledge from your
> actions, you know—if you start to think a lie, you'll end up
> living a lie. And that's what God has allowed to happen, so

that you'll see what the real consequences are. Start out by trying to believe that the creation doesn't proclaim the greatness of our God, and you'll end up by acting as if there's no such thing as the right way to act. You'll be overtaken by envy, malice, and other vices, and you'll become pitiless murderers and worse.

In fact, by making yourself believe a lie about God, you'll leave yourself open to acting out lies in your life. If you're a woman, normally attracted to men, you'll exchange that attraction for an attraction to other women. If you're a man, who desires a woman, you'll find yourself desiring other men instead. That's what it means to deny reality: you end up with nothing real at all about you.

In this passage, as we have paraphrased it, Paul is making a complex argument in which sexual behavior is a secondary point. Much comment on this passage, however, has been attracted to the section about sexual behavior and has made it the main point. But it is not. The main point is the danger of ignoring something that is staring you in the face, but that you don't want to see or refuse to acknowledge. Not only that, you are willing to blind yourself or muddy your thought processes in order to deny it. That is a spiritually dangerous thing to do, Paul argues, because it tends to distort *all* of your thought and action in the long run.

To be sure, on a literal level, what Paul is saying does not and cannot make sense. Idolatrous thought—or disordered thought of any kind—does not cause homosexual attraction. Ignoring reality may be an unwise thing to do, but it doesn't affect our sexual orientation. So what do we do with this passage? Do we simply ignore it, because on the logical level it doesn't make sense?

I think we can derive a surprising lesson from it, and one that does deal with homosexuality, but in a way that would never have occurred to Paul. People who become aware over time that they have a homosexual orientation sometimes react at first in ways that try to deny that reality. Because of social or religious

pressures, they try to behave as heterosexuals—dating members
of the opposite sex, even marrying and having children—and
try to force themselves to believe a lie about themselves. Ultimately, in many cases, it does not work. They may conduct clan-
destine affairs, cheating on their heterosexual partners because
they are not sexually satisfied; they may engage in compulsive
behaviors, like drinking too much, eating too much, or working
too much; and they very often become depressed. Such a situation is unhealthy for the homosexual partner, and equally so for
the (usually unaware) heterosexual one. In fact, both partners
may engage in a complex avoidance of facing the reality of their
lives. The only solution is to acknowledge the truth: for those
who are homosexual, trying to live as if they were heterosexuals is simply to ignore a reality that is staring them in the face. It
introduces distortion, dissembling, and lying into every area of
life, and such distortion is physically, psychologically, and spiritually unhealthy.

That is why, for many of us, recognition of homosexual relationships is a healthy thing. For those who are gay it means not
having to live a lie. For those who are straight, it means not forcing our neighbors to hide a basic fact from us and from themselves. It is, in fact, to love our neighbors as ourselves: to allow
our gay neighbors to do what our straight neighbors can do, up
to and including marrying.

I know that for some readers this line of reasoning will seem
nothing but perverse, to label it so ironically. I have taken a passage from Paul and, seemingly, made it the opposite of what it is
on the surface. But what it is on the surface—which includes
the fact that Paul was not aware that homosexual orientation
could be a fixed aspect of one's personality—is not logical. I hope
it is clear that the argument in Romans 1.18–32 is not one that
we can accept today, but the underlying point is of great spiritual value. To live a lie—to ignore a reality that is directly in front
of you—is spiritually very perilous. That is Paul's main argument,
and in that we can join him wholeheartedly. To use this argument
to force a homosexual person to continue to live a lie is, it seems
to me, a far deeper betrayal of Paul's thought, leading to a far

more perverse result, than the reconsideration that I have undertaken here.

And the larger point of this book also applies. Those who
would wish to use these eight passages—four from the Old Testament and four from the New Testament—as absolute prohibitions of homosexual activity, as justifying second-class status (at
best) within our churches for homosexual persons, and as for-
bidding any efforts to bless homosexual unions or to ordain persons who are in committed homosexual relationships will have
to explain two matters, if they are to be intellectually honest.
First, they will have to explain why passages that are so ambigu-
ous are to be applied as if they were clear and definitive. And
second, and far more difficult, they will have to explain why *these*
passages are to be applied in such a literal way, and the far more
numerous passages having to do with social and economic justice are to be relegated to some distant future or some ideal commonwealth that will never come into being.

AUTHORITY

Who's in Charge Here?

Question: Is the Bible "liberal" or "conservative"?
Answer: Yes.
Alternative answer: No.

IT IS A NATURAL human desire to wish to find in the Bible, or in any source of authority, validation for our views. But, as the somewhat whimsical question-and-answer indicates, the fact of the matter is that the Bible neither uniformly endorses, nor unequivocally refutes, our opinions—no matter what those opinions may be. In addition, as the previous argument has tried to show, we cannot unequivocally endorse all that the Bible says, at least not on the surface. The Bible can be "wrong" about certain things, and this is true whether we are "liberal" or "conservative." So the real question is: how can the Bible be authoritative for us, if the Bible itself can be wrong?

What do we mean when we say that the Bible is an authoritative document for us? In considering this question carefully, we will have to look at what "authority" in general might mean for us, and what happens when authority is present and active.

First, look at the ways in which we speak about authority. Someone can "claim the authority" to do or say something. Someone can "seize the authority" to issue orders—say, in a military coup. We say that we "recognize the authority" of some person or some organization. We may "submit to authority" if we believe or see that we have no choice. Someone may "confer authority" on someone else. And someone can "gain" or "earn" or "attain" authority to direct actions or make decisions—by training, by election or selection, or some other means.

These kinds of statements make one aspect of authority clear: authority is power. It is a relationship between two entities, one of which recognizes and accepts the power of the other in certain respects. In some cases this recognition of authority is forced: someone under arrest, or someone unarmed among those in possession of firearms, may "recognize authority" because there is no alternative. In other cases, the power of the authoritative partner is freely acknowledged. We accept the authority of medical personnel, for example, because we trust their training and expertise. We can leave the hospital or medical office where we are being treated, but we usually do not choose to do so because we accept the authority of the professionals there to carry out their tasks for our benefit—even if those tasks cause us pain, diminished capacity, or discomfort. In still other cases, the authoritative partner has become so over time, by a process of gradual increase of knowledge or experience: someone, for example, who has shown ability in business attains greater managerial authority commensurate with demonstrated results.

Authority, then, is power. But what about submission to authority? Is that merely powerlessness? In some cases, obviously, yes. Someone in jail, or someone performing a task under the direction of someone with a gun, or someone "under the gun" of an overwhelming requirement such as economic necessity is powerless against the authority. But in most cases—as with medical authority—the relationship is not quite so asymmetrical. We can choose a different doctor, decline a course of treatment, and so on. We have some "resistance authority" in the relationship: the authority to decide what is done with our own bodies, for example.

Authority, in other words, in many cases acknowledges the autonomy of the other entity in the relationship. In fact, when exercised properly authority should enhance autonomy: the authority of a teacher, the authority of a manager, the authority

of a government, and many other types of authority are all ideally exercised with the aim of increasing the abilities, and therefore the freedom, of those subject to authority.

Now consider a somewhat different kind of authority. Think
about some major and formative moment in your own life, such
as a significant esthetic experience. Think about a time you stood
before a painting or statue, or heard a great piece of music, or
watched a play or movie, or read a great novel or poem. Try to
remember what that experience was like.

For many people such experiences are at first overwhelming.
The painting or novel or symphony dominates one's consciousness, so that one has little or no awareness of anything else: one
does not exercise any critical judgment; one has no ability to
stand back; one almost has no sense of self. When the experience is over, and normal awareness gradually returns, there is still
the sense that one has been in the presence of superior power.
One is changed, a different person, afterward.

In the same way, we are sometimes overwhelmed by the presence of another person. It may be at the first meeting with someone who will be a lover or a close friend; it may be a revered
teacher. Once again, however, in the presence of the person—
in conversation with them or contemplation of them, in listening to a lecture or participating in a discussion—our awareness
of ourselves and our critical consciousness are muted or absent.
Our awareness is filled with the other, not with ourselves—or
with what the other is saying or doing. Our response is not
something that we consciously will: in effect, it seems to be
"called out" of us, elicited by the presence of the person and
what they are saying, just as our esthetic response to the great
work of art is elicited by the work itself, and is not something we
are deliberately doing.

We can clearly see that this second sort of response, though
it may feel compelled, is in a different category from the submission to authority that characterizes the first acknowledgment
of authority. We submit to the teacher or the police, to the man-
agement of those who are our superiors at our place of employment, or to the government, in part because they exercise

external control over us. The police or the government possess powers that exceed ours by a good deal; the teacher or the employer, while they may not be able to compel our physical presence, can deny us certain benefits—a diploma, a salary—that we need or want. So, in these cases, we remain within the orbit of authority for reasons that are at least partly external to ourselves.

In the case of the other kind of experience, however, we are not compelled in such external ways. We can leave the concert hall, or put down the book—but we don't want to do so. We may stay awake to read past the time when we should be trying to sleep, simply because what we are reading is so important or so attractive to us. We can remove ourselves from the presence of the revered teacher or the beloved, but, once again, we don't want to. Thus, although the experience may feel in some ways more like a compulsion than that of going to work, it is essentially freer, because we find ourselves (when we have leisure to reflect on the experience) doing what we want, not what we must.

It is this kind of response, ideally, that we should make to the authority of the Bible. I think that this is what is meant in Matthew 7.28–29: "Now when Jesus had finished saying these things, the crowds were astounded at his teaching, for he taught them as one having authority, and not as their scribes." The "scribes" were knowledgeable interpreters of the Scriptures, and as such, in Matthew's thought, they represent the external application of the strictures contained in the Bible. Jesus, however, is clearly presented here (the words come at the conclusion of the Sermon on the Mount) as teaching so compellingly that those who hear him accept the teaching because of its intrinsic worth.

Nor should we read this contrast as one between the Old Testament and the New, as if the Old Testament epitomizes the sort of authority that comes by external enforcement, while the New Testament's authority is that of virtue attracting us by its own intrinsic worth. For instance, in Isaiah's vision of the glory of restored Jerusalem (chapters 60–62), the prophet speaks of the pilgrimage that all the inhabitants of the earth shall one day make to Zion:

Arise, shine; for your light has come,
  and the glory of the LORD has risen upon you.
For darkness shall cover the earth,
  and thick darkness the peoples;
but the LORD will arise upon you,
  and his glory will appear over you.
Nations shall come to your light,
  and kings to the brightness of your dawn. (60.1–3)

Like light in the darkness, the glory of the LORD is compelling by its very beauty, and all the people of the earth will be attracted to it. In Jeremiah's great promise of the new covenant (31.31–34), the prophet states (clearly in the context of a covenant with "the house of Israel"): "I will put my law [torah, "teaching"] within them, and I will write it on their hearts; and I will be their God, and they shall be my people."

This does not mean that the Bible's authority can never challenge us. Obviously, we can be changed (for the better, we hope) by a relationship with another in which we are confronted about some behavior or character trait of ours that the other person finds fault with. (Sometimes this fault-finding is explicit, sometimes unstated and simply a matter of being in the presence of a standard that is different from ours.) The Bible certainly has numerous texts that can confront us with standards differing from our own. But what is truly valuable about the Bible's message is our sense that it is communicating to us something about the God who has inspired the text—that the text says something not because the human author simply thought it was a good idea, but because the human author, under a sort of divine pressure, has revealed to us something of the "character" of God by showing us what God values.

This is not easy to ascertain, and many determinations of "what the Bible says with authority" would have to be provisional. In addition, even where all parties are agreed on what the Bible says—for example, that one should care for the poor and needy—there can be disagreement over *how* this care can be expressed.

The process of ascertaining what in the Bible should be accepted—like other aspects of the spiritual life, such as what one should do for employment, what charitable acts to undertake, and so on—is known as discernment. Deciding whether to attend to a particular Bible passage, and how we should do so, is what I would like to turn to next.

How Do We Decide?
This question is a special case of the recurring human one: how do I decide what to do? How do I make a choice that is momentous and, possibly, irreversible once persisted in? The answer in classical Christian thought is that we engage in the process of discernment.

For the purposes of this discussion of how to apply difficult Bible passages, I have divided the process of discernment into three sections, each with three parts. For my own guidance and to help in organizing them, I have also used an ancient mnemonic device: alliteration. Thus, in the first step of discernment, we *compare, consult,* and *consider.* In the second step, we *pause, pray,* and *proffer.* In the third, we *apply, assess,* and *adjust.*

1.a. Compare
We cannot take any passage in the Bible in isolation. We must look at it in the fullest context possible. In this book, we are looking at difficult passages in their own contexts, but also in the context of other difficult passages, to see if one passage suggests to us helpful ways to approach another. This means that we cannot look simply to one verse or passage to determine how we should act, or what moral position we should take. The Bible in its entirety is the context for such a decision; and, what is more, it is the Bible *as a witness to who God is* that is the context. If, after consideration, we determine that a particular view, even if it seems to be rooted in the Bible, is not consonant with who God is, we must abandon that view. It is God who rules, not the Bible.

Example. "Let a woman learn in silence with full submission. I permit no woman to teach or to have authority over a man; she is to keep silent" (1 Timothy 2.11–12). Before we apply such a statement to our current situation, to determine for example that we cannot ordain women or allow women to teach theology to men who will be ordained, we must look elsewhere. Since Jesus had close followers who were women; since women first announced the resurrection of Jesus to men; and since Galatians 3.28 states that "there is no longer Jew or Greek, there is no longer slave or free, there is no longer male and female; for all of you are one in Christ Jesus," we can judge according to our own needs as to whether we wish to accept the full ministry of women.

1.b. Consult

We cannot rely only on our own insights. We must look to others who have spoken or written about the passage or the issue. Most crucially, we must be sure to take into account those whose views might differ markedly from our own. The real test of a position comes not merely when it is validated by those who are in agreement, but when it is tested by, and takes account of, those who disagree. This means that the community context for discernment must be as wide as possible, and we need to make every effort to keep in our community those with whom we disagree. (This point is discussed more fully in the next chapter.)

Example. "What God has joined together, let no one separate" (Mark 10.9). Before we use this verse to forbid any divorce, we need to consult with those whose marriages have failed and who needed to be set free from them. We also need to take into account the changes in lifestyle and the realities of our own world as opposed to the world in which Jesus made this pronouncement. He spoke in response to a question, "Is it lawful for a man to divorce his wife?" (v. 2). A woman who was divorced at that time had few recourses: she could return to her father's house (if he still lived) or to that of another male relative, but if no one would take her in, her prospects were very grim. Besides looking at the experience of others, we have to find out as much as we can about the answer that Jesus intended to give. Perhaps

Perhaps he was concerned that women should be protected from the consequences of divorce in that society.

1.c. Consider

We must patiently sit with the evidence and interpretations we have gathered. This means that we have to weigh these matters with an open mind (and heart) and guard against coming to a conclusion too quickly, or without taking all views into account. Note the following step.

Example. "The children of this age are more shrewd in dealing with their own generation than are the children of light. . . . Make friends for yourselves by means of dishonest wealth" (Luke 16.8–9). Before we take this to mean that we can use the dishonest methods of our surrounding culture, as long as we are doing it in God's service rather than our own, we need to consider the fullness of interpretation of this parable. Ultimately, the point seems to be not "any methods are allowed as long as your goal is all right," but "you should work as hard and as cleverly for good things as the people around you are working for selfish goals."

For the next parts of the discernment process, instead of particular examples for each step, we will take as an example someone who wants to give away the bulk of his or her possessions—perhaps to live quietly in retirement, perhaps to enter a religious vocation, or for whatever reason. "Sell all that you own and distribute the money to the poor" (Luke 18.22).

2.a. Pause

Unnecessary haste in decision-making is the enemy of discernment. To be sure, there are times in life when a decision must be made then and there; but when something—internal or external—seems to be hurrying us to make a decision and there is no reason why it has to be made in a hurry, we need to stop and ask, "What is the urgency?" It will often be the case that the hurry to decide is a way of dodging the difficulties that we do not want to confront, or that others do not want us to consider.

In the case of a decision to give away all of one's property, the momentous character of it should be indication enough that it is not a decision to be undertaken hastily, but rather requires extensive reflection.

2.b. Pray

This may seem obvious, but we should pray about any important decision. Ideally, we should pray all along, but it is when we have gathered information and are at the point of deciding that we can often most profitably pray over it. We are not praying for God to decide for us, nor are we praying in order to give information to God; rather, we are asking for grace to use the time, the information, and our own experience carefully in determining what we will think about a particular passage.

Anyone considering a radical change of life should be asking for guidance from God at every opportunity.

2.c. Proffer

We should offer our decision to others to consider as well. This means discussing it with those whom we trust—and, ideally, with someone trustworthy who may not agree with us but who wishes the best for us.

We need to discuss such a change in our lives with those whom we respect. We also need to discuss it with any others—family members or friends who may be dependent on us—who will be affected by it. They may not have a veto, but unless the circumstances are something like extreme estrangement, they should at least be able to express an opinion before the decision is irrevocable.

3.a. Apply

Then, and only then, should we apply our decision: make the determination, go ahead with the action, or whatever the case may be.

Perhaps we can give away our possessions gradually, rather than all at once, so that we can see how in fact this feels over time.

3.b. Assess

Having gone ahead, we must continue to study the matter. Has our decision resulted in any good or bad consequences? Do we need to take those consequences into account? Are those who love us happy or unhappy about our decision? Are we happy or unhappy? (Note that a decision that makes us unhappy may nevertheless be the right decision; but we are certainly justified in taking happiness—our own or others'—into account in the assessment of any decision. Unhappiness for its own sake is never a good choice.)

If we have not given away our possessions all at once, we can pause periodically and see how things are going—with ourselves and with others.

3.c. Adjust

Depending on what factors we decide to take into account at the assessment stage, we should then adjust our decision. This can be a matter of fine-tuning, or it can, quite frankly, mean the abandonment of the decision and beginning the process over again. Until we have lived with the decision for a time, we will not be able to assess it fully.

The Bible as Witness

If we have gone through a procedure like this when faced with a section or passage of the Bible that we find troubling, we are more likely to be confident in our ultimate decision about the approach to take to that text (whatever that approach might be). Furthermore, we will be less willing to accept the criticism that we are simply jettisoning the Bible when it is inconvenient. Finally, we can be reasonably confident that we have carefully considered all of the relevant approaches to the passage, including those with which we ultimately disagree. It is important to recognize that even after such a careful process our decision can still be provisional, and new evidence, or a new way of considering the old evidence, may bring us to revisit our decision, reconsider it, and after careful thought, change it. But in the absence of such new evidence or approach, we can reasonably act on the decision we have come to.

Such a decision is not necessarily one that avoids any difficulty the Bible puts in our way. It may in fact clear the way for us to put into practice much more challenging parts of the Bible. It is, after all, far easier (if we are not ourselves homosexuals) to condemn homosexual relationships than it is to sell all that we have and give to the poor. It is more pleasant for us, if we live in a society where people like us have many advantages and can live comfortably without resorting to illegal or immoral activity, to condemn as criminals and imprison for long terms all those whose desperation has led them to commit theft or prostitution in order to obtain the illegal drugs that their subsection of society has introduced them to. Yes, it is better not to use drugs; no one should be forced into prostitution either by economic necessity or as a form of slavery; and it is certainly wrong to steal; but that is not the end of the story for those who profess faith in the God of the Bible. Instead of merely proclaiming moral strictures and condemning all who violate them, we may be called to take measures costly to ourselves to reduce the conditions that bring about such violations. We may also see our own practices—such as our reliance on lengthy prison terms as punishment and deterrence for a wide variety of crimes—as subject to judgment in the light of the Bible, as I have tried to show in the chapter on justice. And it seems to me that there is a telling point in the account of Jesus and the rich young man (Matthew 19.16–30; Mark 10.17–31; Luke 18.18–30). Although we are not told until the end of the conversation between Jesus and the man that the man is wealthy, it throws new light on his obedience to the commandments from his youth onwards. What trouble was it to him not to steal or murder or lie or defraud? He had plenty of money, and therefore was not tempted by desperation to do whatever he had to do in order to get enough money to live. And why shouldn't he honor his parents? It may have been because of his parents that he was wealthy. The only sin that Jesus lists that could have tempted him without regard to his money was adultery. But even there, he presumably had the luxury of marrying someone after being given a wide array of choices.

Another advantage of a careful consideration of the passages that cause us trouble—and a refusal to take them simply as "given" and put into practice—is that we are thereby following the practice of the Bible itself, in the Book of Job. One of the lessons we take away from the story of Job is that telling lies—even pious lies, even lies that comport with certain passages of Scripture, even lies designed to put God in the best possible light— is something that God condemns. Pretending that something manifestly unjust is nevertheless what God wants us to do is akin, in this view, to arguing (as Job's friends do) that, because God is righteous, and a righteous being would never inflict suffering on an innocent man, Job must be guilty of something. God would rather, I think, have us argue against something in the Bible on the grounds that God would not have wanted us to do such a thing, rather than do it even though we thought it was unjust, and pretend that it *was* just because God ordered it to be done. God would rather have us say that, as far as we can see, God's actions are unjust, than say that God could never do anything unjust and therefore we must say something that is not true about ourselves. Job's friends, who become his accusers, essentially invite him to lie about his own behavior in their efforts to justify God's actions. Job refuses, even to the point of challenging God to a debate on the topic. When God actually appears, Job is overawed and repents—God's real presence carries its own authority. Nevertheless, after a recital of the power and wonders of creation that does not directly answer Job's question, and after Job's promise of repentance, God turns to the friends and says:

> My wrath is kindled against you . . . for you have not spoken
> of me what is right, as my servant Job has. Now therefore take
> seven bulls and seven rams, and go to my servant Job, and
> offer up for yourselves a burnt offering; and my servant Job
> shall pray for you, for I will accept his prayer not to deal with
> you according to your folly; for you have not spoken of me
> what is right, as my servant Job has done. (42.7–8)

Speaking what is right about God is complicated, once we get beyond abstractions—"God is righteous," for instance—and start dealing with concrete realities. Does God want rebellious sons to be executed? Even the ancient rabbis thought this law should never be carried out. Similarly, does God want anyone who has engaged in homosexual intercourse to be put to death? It is not an abandonment of the Bible—it may in fact be truer to the Bible than a rigid and unthinking acceptance—to argue, on grounds the Bible itself has led us to, that God does not, could not, mean for us to do such a thing. When we say that we accept the authority of the Bible, we are ultimately saying—unless we are idolaters of the text itself—that we accept God's authority, that the Bible is a witness to the character of God, and that we mean to carry out in our lives those actions and teachings that we find in the Bible that fit with the character of the God we worship.

The authority of the Bible, in other words, is not something intrinsic to the Bible itself; it is the authority of a pointer, a witness, that derives its power and importance from the matter it is leading us to. And God is what the Bible leads us to. That means, ultimately, that reading the Bible is more an act of coming to know a person than it is an act of coming to understand an argument. Logic, intellectual effort, and understanding have their place, as they do when we come to know people we have met. We learn about their backgrounds, we compare what they said on one occasion with what they said on another, we try to see more deeply into what they mean as we listen to what they say. In the same way, when we read the Bible we do not abandon our intellectual abilities. But we are not, if we are reading as Christians, only reading with intellectual interest. We are not reading only with the goal of knowing some*thing*. We are also reading with the aim of knowing some*one*.

This leads to the final point, and the need for one further chapter that is not, strictly speaking, about the Bible at all. We come to know people one by one, but we often meet people in the context of larger groups. We meet people when we join a community, and we come to know individuals as parts of the community, not only as persons on their own. Bible reading is undertaken, for Christians, not only as a solitary activity—though it can be done as part of individual prayer, meditation, and learning—but also as a group activity, in worship and preaching. So we must take a look at the character of the community in which Bible reading takes place. What is the Christian church, and what are its characteristics? That is the topic on which we will end our meditations.

COMMUNITY

Will We Ever Get Along?

THE BIBLE FOR Christians is a foundational part of who we are. For some it is "the Bible alone" that is the basis of their Christian community; for others, the Bible as explained or mediated through some aspect of their tradition—the historic creeds, the teaching authority of the church, the prayers of the gathered community—forms the context in which they understand themselves. In whatever way each group defines it, however, the Bible is a crucial part of who they are and how they see themselves. We therefore must ask ourselves: what effect will our view of the Bible have on how we exist as a Christian community? Have we undermined our very existence by questioning whether the Bible is right about various matters of morality, social relations, or law? Are we at risk of building on a shaky foundation—on something that will give way if we press it too hard?

Can a community continue to exist, with its members in relationship with each other, if they disagree about things? Once we have asked the question, we can see that the issue is one of determining what is central and what is peripheral in a community's beliefs. Different communities are going to draw their borders in different places. For some, those who dissent even from beliefs that are not a part of the core doctrine cannot be considered full members of the community. For others, there needs to be a wide tolerance of diversity of opinion, because only when there is such tolerance can we be sure that the truth will eventually come forth. For some, truth is a matter of official pronouncement: the teaching of recognized, duly constituted authorities, or the Bible as interpreted according to a specific method. For others, insight can arise from various quarters, not only through official channels, and must be considered by the full community, without rushing to decide prematurely about whether a belief or a practice should be acceptable or not.

Defined communities of the first sort can theoretically, at least, make decisions about membership fairly easily. Those who wish to be a part of the community must ascribe to all the teaching that the community itself has decided is central. Such teaching can extend far beyond central doctrines like belief in God or standard practices like Sunday worship; it can take in diet (fasting or abstaining), defining acceptable marriage partners, economic practices (required tithing), and so on. Those who do not agree, or who do not wish to adopt the required practices, are encouraged or even forced to leave. Sometimes the strictures extend beyond doctrine or practice to take in prohibitions on discussing certain topics. When individuals make the decision to join such a community, or to remain within it, they at least implicitly accept the conditions of membership and accede to the full list of beliefs and practices. Once they have done so, many aspects of their lives and beliefs require no further consideration. These things have been decided and they are done with.

Few communities in today's world, at least in developed countries, can be quite so strict about their membership. With the possible exception of those groups who largely withdraw from contact with outsiders—Amish groups, certain Orthodox Jewish communities, or subsets of larger communities like monastic orders—the boundaries of almost any community are a bit fuzzy. This description is of a pure or ideal community according to certain criteria, not necessarily a description of any actual church or denomination.

In the second sort of community—one where differing views are tolerated, and where questions about beliefs are freely discussed—there is a different approach to understanding the character of the community itself. We can approach this view of community in two different ways: working out from the Bible, and working forward from a formulation in one of the historic creeds of some Christian churches. We will then see if these ways of working toward an understanding of community are compatible, and even if they essentially end up in the same place.

Early Christian Communities
The New Testament has two central depictions of the character of the Christian community. These are in the Acts of the Apostles and in the major letters that follow the Book of Acts. In each there is a summary or distillation of the community's character: in Acts we have Luke's list of the distinguishing marks of the early Christians, and in his first letter to the Corinthians Paul uses the metaphor of the body to describe the nature of the church.

Luke describes the early Christians in this way:

> [Those who became members of the community through baptism] devoted themselves to the apostles' teaching and fellowship, to the breaking of bread and the prayers.... All who believed were together and had all things in common; they would sell their possessions and goods and distribute the proceeds to all, as any had need. (Acts 2.42, 44–45)

The characteristics of the community, therefore, were: teaching, fellowship, worship, and care for one another.

Not one of these characteristics presumes a uniform approach. The apostles were severely divided in their teachings about admission of non-Jews to the community, a difference that it took years to resolve. The council convened by James, the head of the church in Jerusalem, reduced the requirements for non-Jews to four: no eating of meat sacrificed to idols, no eating of blood, no eating of "what is strangled" (that is, carrion or meat from an animal not slaughtered according to kosher precepts, which required the blood to be drained from the living animal), and no fornication (Acts 15.29). In Galatians 2.10, however, Paul's account of this claims that "they asked only one thing, that we remember the poor." There is no mention of dietary restrictions. Paul goes on to say that he continued to argue with Peter about eating with non-Jews (2.11–14). Clearly, then, "fellowship" was compatible with strong differences about practices and beliefs.

In 1 Corinthians 12.14–26, Paul develops the metaphor of the body as representing the character of the community. He is here borrowing a recognized analogy from Greco-Roman thought, in which the "body" of citizens is compared to the human body—under the rule of mind the limbs act for defense, the stomach feeds the whole body, and so on, just as the rulers direct the army and the agricultural laborers provide food for all. Paul, however, is not concerned to develop a point-for-point analogy with different parts of the human body and different groups within the church. His point is different, and more subtle: just as the body needs the great variety of organs and limbs in order to function to its fullest extent—and just as a body that consisted entirely of one kind of organ would not really be a body at all—so the community needs as many different kinds of members as it can possibly get, and not all of them can be "honorable" (that is, decent to be seen in public—he is clearly thinking of the elimination of waste from the body). If anything, this is a plea to include as many different kinds of people and as much variety as possible, so that the community can function as it ought to do.

In effect, then, we are given in the New Testament clear indications that the community must not merely tolerate, but should welcome, a wide range of people and views within the group. Uniformity is not held up as an ideal. Variety is. And where unity appears, it is the unity of those united to Christ in a relationship that is personal, not doctrinal, as in Ephesians: "the unity of the faith [trust] and of the [personal] knowledge of the Son of God, to maturity, to the measure of the full stature of Christ" (4.13).

The witness of the Bible to the character of the Christian community, therefore, is one of a group accepting a wide variety of persons as members. To understand how this might work in practice, we can turn to a formulation of the character of the church that is given in the historic text of the Nicene Creed, which many Christians recite on a regular basis.

Opposing Ideals

The creed is primarily concerned with avowing the nature of God as Trinity and Jesus Christ as Son of God. Near the end, however, comes the phrase that we will examine more closely: the expression of belief in the "one, holy, catholic, and apostolic church."

What do these words mean? Should they convey anything distinct, or are they merely an ancient formula? A tiny minority of those who repeat those words may understand what they meant to those who first formulated them, but can others use that as guidance for what they might mean? Or should they try to reconsider these characteristics in the light of the present experience of the Christian community?

The bishops who ratified these words may have had their disagreements, but probably not about this statement. The church was "one"—that is, united (administratively and intellectually) in faith and theology; "holy," or sacred, as something dedicated to God and therefore God's possession; "catholic," covering (potentially) the whole known, inhabited world; and "apostolic," tracing its lineage and teaching back to those followers of Jesus who by witnessing his resurrection and receiving the Holy Spirit as his gift had been anointed apostles, and had passed on their apostolic authority to their successors, the bishops of God's undivided, universal church.

We are a long way from the ecclesiastical reality of the Councils of Nicaea and Constantinople. Institutional divisions are not even the primary difficulty; there are, underlying the separate church bodies to which we belong, very different visions of what the church is; what unity might consist in; where the sacred is found; what a claim to universality might mean in our multicultural, multireligious world; or what it means to stand in the tradition of the apostles. For some, the church is a voluntary group that one joins like any other organization, when one basically agrees with what it says or likes those who already belong to it. For others, the church is the relatively small group whom God has chosen as representatives on earth, and to whom God has granted eternal life, while all others—not only adherents of non-Christian religions, but even large numbers of those claiming to be Christian—are excluded forever. Some, in affirming the church as "one, holy, catholic, and apostolic," would enforce a uniformly understood theology on all its members; others would try to accommodate as wide an understanding as possible, containing diverse and even opposing views within the group. And there are many positions between these extremes.

I propose that we try a different approach to understanding this phrase. I do so with the full knowledge that what I am suggesting is not what the originators of the formula meant by it, and may not be what most contemporaries mean by it, either. But the creed, if it is to continue as a unifying constituent of common belief, has to be a living expression of a vital trust; it cannot require adherence to modes of thought that no longer correspond to reality.

Here, therefore, is how I understand the Christian community as being "one, holy, catholic, and apostolic." The church—the community of Christians, either in one place and time or spread throughout the world and throughout history—is "one" and "holy" *but also* "catholic" and "apostolic."

I believe that the community of Christians is both one and catholic. That is, I believe that it exists in the creative tension between oneness with our Lord Jesus Christ and a diversity of inclusion that takes in (potentially) any who wish to be a part of it. There cannot be a decision that excludes anybody except the decision of Jesus Christ:

> This is my commandment, that you love one another as I
> have loved you. . . . I do not call you servants any longer,
> because the servant does not know what the master is doing;
> but I have called you friends, because I have made known to
> you everything that I have heard from my Father. You did not
> choose me but I chose you. And I appointed you to go and
> bear fruit. (John 15.12, 15–16)

"I have called you friends. . . . You did not choose me but I chose you." It is Jesus' decision whom to call; we can respond or not, but it is not up to us to assess the validity of someone else's call. Nevertheless, the community that Jesus calls together is not merely a heterogeneous assembly—it is, and must be, unified around the one who called it into being. Jesus calls us into relationship with him; that is our unity. Jesus calls us to be a part of his community because of our very differences, differences that will only grow as we become more and more the persons God intends us to be; that is our catholicity.

The implications of this tension mean that we, as members of the church that is both one and catholic, must hold simultaneously to two ideals that can be in opposition in our imperfect world. We must simultaneously work toward the maximum of diversity and the closest of unity. Unity, therefore, does not mean uniformity. But diversity does not mean heterogeneity. We are called to accept those with whom we disagree, but we are also called to acknowledge that within the community not everything can be a matter of "anything goes." Some things do make a difference. We cannot simply affirm our commitment to Jesus while acting as if that commitment should have no effect on what we do; nor can such a commitment merely imply that we are free to accept any content that we find it convenient to pour into it. For those who wish to emphasize the inclusivity of the community, it may be necessary to work hard to take into account where the limits of inclusion are, and for those who wish to be clear about what membership in the community means, and who therefore is not included, it may be necessary to work hard to make those limits as broad and inclusive as possible. Each side, in other words, is challenged to work in opposition to its own instinctive impulse. Full membership in the community, of necessity, will have to imply the willingness to consider those who are at the opposite pole from us to be members also—even those on the opposite pole from us on the central issue of *who* is to be included. Thus, until the final consummation of our encounter with God, "one" and "catholic" are, and must remain, the opposing ideals of unity and inclusiveness. For us these ideals will sometimes—perhaps often—be at odds. Only God can resolve them. And since this is God's task, not ours, we should not take steps to preempt God's proper function, nor should we arrogate it to ourselves.

In a similar way, I think we must understand more broadly what it means when we say that the church is both "holy" and "apostolic." "Holiness" is the quality of being "set apart," and God is the holy being above all other holy beings. God is apart from all the cosmos that God has created, and God cannot be identified with that cosmos or with any part of it.

"Apostolicity" is the character of being "sent out" into the world that is apart from God. To be an apostle means to be in the world—"Then Jesus called the twelve together and gave them power and authority over all demons and to cure diseases, and he sent them out to proclaim the kingdom of God and to heal" (Luke 9.1–2; see also Matthew 10.1–14; Mark 6.6–13). But it means to be in the world in a particular way:

> If you belonged to the world, the world would love you as its
> own. Because you do not belong to the world, but I have
> chosen you out of the world—therefore the world hates you.
> (John 15.19)

That is, God calls us both to be set apart from the world and to be working within the world—both set apart as God's possession and sent out by God to God's own world. These two aspects of our existence as the Christian community are polar opposites, and will often be in conflict. The apartness of the community is necessary if it is to have any effect when it is in the world—in other words, its apostolic effectiveness depends on its holy apartness. Once again, there is a creative tension between these poles, and there is a necessity for recognizing that in our world they may not be completely reconcilable.

Different groups have put the emphasis at different points along the spectrum between these poles at different times and places in Christian history. Some groups, like the old order Amish, withdraw as completely as possible from the world; some groups within larger church bodies, like Trappists, withdraw while still remaining part of a community that is in the world. Other groups, like established churches, have identified more or less with worldly communities. The church can become so identified with the world in which it exists that it makes no difference to that world; it can so differentiate itself from the world that it has virtually no contact with it, and therefore no effect on it. The difficult, dangerous, but necessary path is to follow the Lord Jesus Christ and live fully within the world, while working to be Jesus' instruments for its transformation into something other than what it is—something that is closer to what Jesus has called it to be.

A Conflict of Goods

We have encountered this sort of polarity elsewhere, if we have tried seriously to live according to our highest ideals. It is a conflict of goods, and it is—or would seem to be—an inevitable part of being fully human, yet finite, in a world that has not yet come to its completeness in God. Biblical writers were well aware of this conflict. Psalm 85.10 reads, for instance (in the translation of the Book of Common Prayer, 1979): "Mercy and truth are met together, righteousness and peace have kissed each other." In this verse the author gives us a brief glimpse of life as it should be and—we hope—life as it will be. The contradictions and compromises that are sadly necessary in our lives will be finally resolved, and all goodness will be fully expressed.

All four Hebrew words that are the keys to this verse—mercy, truth, righteousness, and peace—represent important concepts, and occur hundreds of times in the Hebrew Bible. Those words are *chesed, emeth, tsedeq,* and *shalom.*

Chesed, here translated "mercy," is the love or kindness that we show when we wish to do the greatest good for another. It is more than the emotion of *feeling* love for another; it emphasizes the loving *actions* we can take on another's behalf. Positively, it means the strength of goodness or love extended toward another; negatively, it is the forbearance that refrains from causing another unnecessary pain. It is usually translated by phrases such as "steadfast love" or, in older translations, "loving-kindness" (which goes back to William Tyndale in the early six-teenth century).

Emeth, "truth," is the quality in a person or an idea that is sta-ble, reliable, or trustworthy—what a person can count on. "Truth" is above all something that will not give way when we press it. It is, in the moral sense, "firm." The word *emeth* is related to the statement of assent at the end of a prayer, *amen,* "truly."

Tsedeq, "righteousness" or "justice," means what is right, nor-mal, or fair. Weights and measures that are *tsedeq* are honest or accurate; kings who are *tsedeq* judge fairly in administering the laws; speech or action that is *tsedeq* is morally true. In general, righteousness means to be in tune with God's justice, the stan-dard of what is honest, true, and moral.

Shalom is that quality of wholeness or soundness that charac-terizes healthy relationships. *Shalom* is not merely the absence of war or conflict; it is a positive state where all parts of the com-munity—whether a community of persons, a community of nations, or the deep community between God and humanity—are fully engaged with each other to the benefit of all.

In combining these ideas in one verse, the psalm refers to experiences that are all too common: the difficulty or impossi-bility of being both merciful and truthful, both morally upright and committed to the deep bonds of peace that should unite any group. In our day-to-day lives, when we need to tell someone a painful truth, mercy sometimes gets put aside. We all know this full well when someone is telling *us* a truth that we need to hear but are trying to avoid. When we tell another a difficult truth, or when we hear a hard truth from someone else, we may very well have the experience of hearing or speaking truth without mercy. Just as bad, if we opt to be merciful we can sometimes unwisely shade the truth, and if someone else is telling us something in a too-kindly way, we may fail to hear the truth we need.

In the same way, when groups that are oppressed demand jus-tice, the effort to carry out justice in historically unjust circum-stances can make matters anything but peaceful. The history of the civil rights struggle in this country provides many examples of the difficulty of peaceful change in the face of relentless hostility, as does the struggle for women's rights. And we in the Anglican Communion, as well as our brothers and sisters in other denominations, know well that treating our fellow Christians with love and justice, and accepting all people, straight and gay, as full members of the Christian fellowship, can provoke very unpeaceful responses from those who oppose us. It is sadly true that those who benefit from oppression can demand peace—peace in the form of "law and order"—in order to stifle legitimate cries for justice.

What this psalm is holding out for us, therefore, is the vision of a world in which the full measure of truth is always merciful, and mercy is never less than fully truthful. And it also envisions a world where justice is not achieved at the expense of peace, nor is peace anything less than the full provision of justice for all. God's promise to us is that we will come to live in a world where righteousness is the very expression of perfect peace, and where the absolute truth is nothing less than the perfection of love.

This is a vision of the ultimate reign of God. It is only then that those good qualities that we unfortunately have to experience as opposites can be reconciled. Mercy—the ability to be tender with another—and truth—the correct alignment of our thoughts with reality—will meet. Righteousness and peace— the quest for justice and the quest for concord—can also often, in our experience, be mutually exclusive. It is only in God's time that these opposites will come into alignment.

When God has fully claimed us all, the conflict of goods will cease. Perhaps we will all desire the truth above all things, and our egos will be out of the way so that "the truth hurts" will no longer be a proverb among us. Or perhaps we will all experience the truth as the most merciful choice. In the same way, in God's reign a truly just order will also be a truly peaceful one. And as with these matters, so it will be with our community characteristics. Now, in our broken and imperfect world, we can only hope for a true unity in diversity, and a real presence in the world while remaining Christ's own forever. But in God's good time, we may trust, we will be blessed with the full reconciliation that

God has promised; and we further trust that such a reconciliation will include resolving conflicting goods.

Perhaps an analogy from everyday life will help to draw out the implications of this. A person may have several friends, and each of those may see a different aspect of their common friend. There may be little overlap: one person may share musical tastes with her friend, while another shares a love of cooking or a favorite writer or a life history or any number of other things. The friends may not know of each other, or, even if they do, they may not particularly get along with each other. They cannot, however, completely disagree about the character of the person whose friendship they have in common, whatever else they may disagree about. If they were so to disagree, something would be wrong: one or both of them would have to be mistaken about the character of their friend.

Another implication follows from this analogy. Though the friends may not like each other, the person whose friendship they share need not, and should not, let that influence how she regards either of them. To the statement, "I don't know what you see in her," the only correct answer is, "But I do." And to the statement, "If you don't stop being friends with him, I won't be friends with you," the only possible moral response is, "I can't end my friendship on the basis of emotional blackmail." In other words, we may choose to withdraw our friendship from someone for our own reasons, but if someone asks us to end a friendship with someone else, we cannot with integrity do anything but refuse. And no true friend would force such a choice upon another, unless the relationship of which she disapproved was of so toxic a kind that the friend herself was becoming a different and lesser person.

No matter how much we may disapprove of someone's friendship with another, therefore, our primary focus should be who she is, not whom she knows. If he or she is still the same person that we have always loved and honored, her friendship or his relationship with someone we cannot bring ourselves to like is not a sufficient reason for us to end our relationship with her.

How does this apply to our lives in the Christian community? We must take the view that any member of that community is there because she or he has a relationship with Jesus. To think so is not to be sentimental or evangelical; it is to be biblical. That relationship—the one between Jesus and each one of us—is the primary one. Any effort on our part to rid the community of a specific person, therefore, must be undertaken with the utmost reluctance and in full knowledge that we may be going against Jesus' desires. And if this is true of a decision about the inclusion of a particular person within the community, how much more is it true of a decision about the inclusion of an entire group?

The tension in this state of affairs is very clearly presented in two sayings of Jesus that seem, on the surface at least, to be incompatible. In Mark 9.39–41, Jesus tells his followers, who have tried to prevent someone from healing in Jesus' name:

Do not stop him; for no one who does a deed of power in my name will be able soon afterward to speak evil of me. Whoever is not against us is for us. For truly I tell you, whoever gives you a cup of water to drink because you bear the name of Christ will by no means lose the reward.

The call of Jesus here is to be expansively inclusive, to welcome any and all who are working toward the same goals, and by all means not to frustrate or separate ourselves from any such person.

In Matthew 12.25–37, Jesus, disputing with the Pharisees, takes a hard line toward those who will observe his good deeds, healings, and so on, and yet condemn him as acting with demonic power. In verse 30, Jesus says to them, "Whoever is not with me is against me, and whoever does not gather with me scatters." Here, Jesus is calling attention to the need to be honest about where the source of our commitment lies, and with whom we have entered into relationship. The statement is a warning: when you see something good being done, do not denigrate the motives of the person you are observing. To do so is to separate yourself from the community, to blaspheme "against the Holy Spirit" (vv. 31–32). The community is clear that everyone who is within the community is there by virtue of their relationship with Jesus Christ through the Holy Spirit; but the community can also honor, and work together with, those who may not yet have the clear light of faith in Jesus, but who want to do the best they can to carry out the will of a righteous God.

The seeming contradiction between the statements, therefore, comes not from their intrinsic meaning but from the situations they are addressing. No one who is doing what is right should be excluded from the community, because the members of the community are not in a position to determine what the person's motives are; and furthermore, those who presume to be able to determine motivation in that way—who say, in effect, "He is doing the right thing, but his motives are evil"—are by that very statement excluding themselves from the community. Motivation is known only to God, and therefore only God can judge our actions according to our motivations; we ourselves are left only with our ability to see the worth of someone's actions, and those we must accept at face value.

What does this have to do with our current impasse about the inclusion of gay and lesbian persons in the Christian community? One thing it should cause us to think about—and this goes for those on either side of the argument—is that the attribution of (usually bad) motivation for people's beliefs should form no part of any argument. Accusing someone of homophobia should be ruled out; likewise, accusations of trendiness or of advocating "if it feels good, do it" should be disallowed. Proponents on either side who make those sorts of accusations should be criticized *by those on their own side:* the issue should be fought out on its merits, and not according to the presumed motivations of those arguing for one side or the other.

The painful decision about who is to be included, and who is to be excluded, from the community of faithful followers of Jesus is the point at which we find ourselves in the Anglican Communion. Some parts of the Communion have decided to take a position that homosexual persons will be treated as full members of the community, with all rights and responsibilities that other members have. Other parts of the Communion have essentially stated that this decision automatically removes those groups, and that the Communion itself is bound to recognize that it has been thus divided. The conflict cannot finally be resolved by anything short of the conversion of one side to the same view as the other side; there is no "middle position" on the particular issue that it is possible to take. Homosexual persons are either equal to other persons, or they are not. To include them but accord them a separate status—communicants but not ordained persons, communicants only if celibate, or some other formula—is precisely to maintain that they are not equal to others.

The best outcome, in my view, is that each side should continue to maintain its position, and continue to discuss it with the other, while continuing to cooperate on every other matter on which we can agree: the reduction of world poverty, the movement toward sustainable development, just allocation of the world's resources, and so on.

Since, however, the position of those opposed to the inclusion of homosexual persons is that they cannot remain part of a Communion that includes those of the opposite view—and since, further, various bishops from around the world and other members of the international Anglican institutional structure have been moving toward the position that there must be some sort of division in the Communion to separate out those who take the inclusive view—we are probably beyond the point where continuing dialogue and full communion are still viable. So we, in the U.S. Episcopal Church and in other parts of the Communion that agree on the full inclusion of homosexual persons, must determine what position we should take.

I would propose that, in keeping with our creedal affirmation of the church as "one, holy, catholic, and apostolic," we adopt the following position. We acknowledge the difference between our views, and we regret the position on the other side that is forcing a split between us. But we will not participate in that split. Whether you recognize us as a part of the Communion or not, we believe that we are still a part of Christ's church; and we further believe that you are a part of Christ's church, as well. We believe that you are wrong about this issue; but we are willing to keep talking with you, and to stay in communion with you, despite our view that you are wrong. We are not going to try to push you out, even though you are trying to push us out. And, if you succeed in pushing us out, we will still recognize you as a part of us, even if you refuse to recognize us as having a part in you.

To follow Paul's exhortation, "Let the same mind be in you that was in Christ Jesus" (Philippians 2.5), we need to internalize what follows:

> who... emptied himself,
>> taking the form of a slave,
>> being born in human likeness.
> And being found in human form,
>> he humbled himself
>> and became obedient to the point of death—
>> even death on a cross. (2.6–8)

The cross of division, of exclusion, may be ours to bear for the time. We are not bearing it alone. It is Jesus Christ who leads the way into the kingdom, followed by every one of those whom Christ has called, each one having taken up the cross. The triumphal procession may look like the journey of criminals to the gallows; but we should long since have come to recognize that the Lamb that was slain—the utterly self-giving love that does not stop giving itself even when dying—is the true ruling power of the universe (Revelation 5.6–14). If we trust in that love, nothing can separate us from it, and that love, long after our divisions have been laid to rest in the grave, will reign forever.

FURTHER READING

Richard Bauckham and Carl Mosser, eds., *The Gospel of John and Christian Theology* (Grand Rapids: William B. Eerdmans Publishing Company, 2008); see especially "John and the Jews."

Adele Berlin and Marc Zvi Brettler, eds., *The Jewish Study Bible* (New York: Oxford University Press, 2004).

William P. Brown, ed., *Engaging Biblical Authority: Perspectives on the Bible as Scripture* (Louisville: Westminster John Knox Press, 2007).

Walter Brueggemann, *Praying the Psalms* (Winona, Minn.: St. Mary's Press, Christian Brothers Publications, 1993); see especially the chapter "Vengeance: Human and Divine."

William N. Eskridge, Jr., and Darren R. Spedale, *Gay Marriage: What We've Learned from the Evidence* (New York: Oxford University Press, 2006).

Luke Timothy Johnson, *The Creed: What Christians Believe and Why It Matters* (New York: Doubleday, 2003).

William Stacy Johnson, *A Time to Embrace: Same-Gender Relationships in Religion, Law, and Politics* (Grand Rapids: William B. Eerdmans Publishing Company, 2006).

Amy-Jill Levine, *The Misunderstood Jew* (San Francisco: HarperSanFrancisco, 2006).

Donn Morgan, *Fighting with the Bible* (New York: Church Publishing, 2007).

Jack Rogers, *Jesus, the Bible, and Homosexuality: Explode the Myths, Heal the Church* (Louisville: Westminster John Knox Press, 2006).

John Shelby Spong, *The Sins of Scripture* (San Francisco: HarperSanFrancisco, 2005).

Phyllis Trible, *God and the Rhetoric of Sexuality* (Philadelphia: Fortress Press, 1978) and *Texts of Terror* (Philadelphia: Fortress Press, 1984).

Dan O. Via and Robert A. J. Gagnon, *Homosexuality and the Bible: Two Views* (Minneapolis: Fortress Press, 2003).

N. T. Wright, *The Last Word: Beyond the Bible Wars to a New Understanding of the Authority of Scripture* (San Francisco: HarperSanFrancisco, 2005).

Erich Zenger, *A God of Vengeance?* (Louisville: Westminster John Knox Press, 1996).

A GUIDE FOR STUDY
AND DISCUSSION

SESSION 1
GENERAL CONSIDERATIONS
Discussion of Chapter 1

Main Point: Interpretation
The Bible needs interpretation, though people disagree about which passages and how they should be understood. For example, it contains contradictory commands that cannot be simply explained away or ignored, but must be dealt with in some way. The Bible also contains ideas, recommendations, and exhortations that we no longer agree with, though people disagree on what these are and how to deal with them.

As soon as we begin to study the Bible, we encounter several kinds of difficulties in interpretation:

- We cannot understand what the passage is saying.
- We think we understand it, but it may be influenced by cultural values that are very different from ours. We may disagree with it, and find it distasteful, immoral, or otherwise not in agreement with our values.
- We can understand the passage and are sympathetic to its underlying values, but it is exhorting us to do things that are impossible.

◆ We can understand and agree with the passage, but carrying it out in any systematic way is simply beyond our capabilities.

Questions
Look up the following Bible passages:

◆ Genesis 49.8–12 *(a blessing on Judah)*
◆ Judges 11.29–40 *(Jephthah's vow)*
◆ Joshua 6.17–21, 8.18–29 *(on conquered cities)*
◆ Matthew 5.42 *(give to anyone who asks)*
◆ Matthew 6.25–34 *(do not worry)*.

Which kind(s) of the difficulties identified above do you find with each one?

How would you interpret these passages in order to come to terms with these difficulties?

Main Point: Types of Language
When studying the Bible it is also important to realize that different parts of the Bible have to be read in different ways, depending on what types of material they are. The Bible, like other literary works, uses language in various ways to talk about one thing while meaning something else, and is not always meant to be taken literally. These ways include:

◆ *metaphor:* being "born again" or "anew" (John 3.1–4)
◆ *irony:* those who pray ostentatiously "have received their reward" (Matthew 6.5)
◆ *parable:* comparing God's kingdom to a shrub (Mark 4.30–32)
◆ *allegory:* comparing God's relationship to Israel to an owner's relationship to a vineyard (Isaiah 5.1–6).

There are any number of clues that the text is using language in nonliteral ways:

- The passage makes no sense when read literally: "They have washed their robes and made them white in the blood of the Lamb" (Revelation 7.14).

- The larger context of the passage contains obvious exaggerations, contradictions, or other indicators of nonhistorical literature: In the book of Jonah, when the great city of Nineveh is threatened with God's judgment, the king issues a decree that all the people *and all the animals* should repent by fasting and wearing sackcloth (Jonah 3.7–8).

- The passage has dream scenes or other clearly fanciful passages: In the Song of Songs, we read, "I slept, but my heart was awake. Listen! My beloved is knocking." The passage which follows is likely a dream sequence, and not a real incident (Song of Songs 5.2–8).

- The passage is clearly fiction—though told for a reason (which may not be the reason that seems obvious to us): The Book of Job begins with a man, Job, who is given no ancestors (unlike almost every other character in the Hebrew Bible), and moves right from the man and his possessions to a scene in heaven (Job 1.1–12).

Questions

Look up the following passages and consider whether they should be read literally, or as some other form of language:

- Judges 9.8–15 *(Jotham on the monarchy)*
- 1 Kings 8.62–63 *(Solomon's offerings)*
- Matthew 17.1–8 *(the Transfiguration)*
- Matthew 18.8–9 *(stumbling blocks)*.

What clues did you look for in the process of determining what form of language each passage might be?

What difference does the form of language make in how you understand these passages?

SESSION 2
VENGEANCE AND ENEMIES
Discussion of Chapters 2 and 3

Main Points

Even when the commands found in the Bible seem straightforward and clear, the ways in which we *apply* the Bible's rules in our own lives may not be immediately obvious. We need to think carefully about how we will apply particular rules that the Bible says we should follow. We cannot always carry them out directly, and when they are phrased in general terms we must think through how we will apply them in particular circumstances.

In some cases the Bible begins by presenting normal (though flawed or even sinful) human behavior, and even seems to be endorsing or commanding it, but later texts in the Bible will contradict those views. We have to look at the wider context and decide *on grounds that are found elsewhere in the Bible* that we will not take the Bible's lead and behave in those particular ways.

Questions

1. When the Bible contains contradictory commands or versions of a story, sometimes later writers or translators attempt to synthesize or reinterpret the details.

Look up the following passages:

- Exodus 12.9, Deuteronomy 16.7, and 2 Chronicles 35.11–13 *(on how the Passover lamb is to be prepared)*
- Deuteronomy 25.5–6 and Leviticus 18.16 *(on succession)*
- Matthew 19.3–12 and 1 Corinthians 7.12–15 *(on divorce)*
- Matthew 5.14–16 *(let your light shine)* and Matthew 6.3–4 *(give alms in secret)*
- Acts 9.1–9 (especially verse 7) and Acts 22.4–11 (especially verse 9) *(on the conversion of Paul)*.

How did biblical writers and later commentators attempt to synthesize these contradictions?

How would you make sense of them?

What contradictory passages have troubled you in your own reading of the Bible?

2. The Bible is by no means uniform in its views of how we deal with questions of violence and revenge, hatred and misunderstandings, peace and war. Even Jesus himself seems to offer contradictory teachings on these matters.

Look up the following passages.

- Exodus 21.22–25, Leviticus 24.19–20, Deuteronomy 19.21, Matthew 5.38–42 *(an eye for an eye)*
- Matthew 5.39 *(do not resist an evildoer)* and Luke 20.9–19 *(vengeance on the wicked tenants)*
- Matthew 10.34–39 and Matthew 26.51–53 *(swords)*.

How do these and other teachings in the Bible inform your thinking on the use of force?

SESSION 3
JUSTICE
Discussion of Chapter 4

Main Points
There is a direct link in the Bible between *justice*—the rules by which we live, whether criminal, economic, or social—and *righteousness*—our moral nature. The biblical texts attempt to bring about communities of human beings who are righteous, communities in which people act with justice not because they are obeying a set of external laws, but because they are righteous people who want to behave in ways that conform to the will of God.

Questions
1. Look up the following passages describing some of the principles of justice in the Bible:

- Leviticus 19.15 *(evenhandedness)*
- Deuteronomy 15.7–11 *(care for the needy)*
- Isaiah 10.1–4 *(denunciation of those who use the law to oppress the needy)*
- Amos 2.6–8 *(punishment of those who exploit the poor)*
- Micah 6.6–8 *(what God really requires).*

In what ways do our current criminal laws, which include the death penalty, long prison sentences, and the imposition of fines but exclude mutilation and humiliation, express or contradict biblical principles?

How would you reform our current system in light of these biblical principles?

How would you decide which biblical principles to adopt or adapt or ignore?

2. Look up these passages that describe some of the Bible's economic principles:

+ Leviticus 19.9–10 *(providing for the destitute)*
+ Leviticus 25.8–17 *(the Jubilee, in which all property returns to its original owners)*
+ Amos 8.4–12 *(the punishment of economic oppressors)*
+ Luke 16.19–31 *(rich man and Lazarus)*
+ Acts 2.44–45; 4.32, 34–37; 5.1–6 *(sharing of possessions, and the consequences of not sharing)*
+ James 2.1–7, 14–17; 5.1–6 *(the sins of the rich and the duty to care for the poor).*

In what ways does our current economic system express or contradict biblical principles?

What does the Bible tell us about our responsibilities for contributing to the welfare of others in our communities?

How could we be better stewards of our resources, as individuals and as communities?

SESSION 4
TREATING THE MARGINALIZED
Discussion of Chapters 5 and 6

Main Points

The Bible itself is not always fair to those who are "marginal" in its own terms, especially women, Jews (in the New Testament), and slaves, but most texts tell us not to marginalize those who are different (resident aliens), those who are poor, and those who are socially disadvantaged, such as widows and orphans. Who is marginal changes with the context, but the Bible's principles about how we treat those who are marginal should not.

Questions

1. Who are the marginalized in our society today? Who are the marginalized in your particular community? in your congregation? Why and how are they marginalized? How do you participate, wittingly or unwittingly, in their marginalization?

What do think the Bible would have to say about those who are marginalized in your congregation, and how they are treated by the larger community?

2. The word "immoral" for us tends to mean "sexually immoral": "living in sin" has traditionally meant "living in an irregular sexual relationship," rather than living in any immoral manner—by extortion, fraud, robbery, exploiting the less fortunate, or any number of other possibilities.

Look up the following passages and consider what they tell us about how the Bible views immorality:

- ◆ Mark 7.20–23 *(the evil that comes from within)*
- ◆ Deuteronomy 27.15–26 *(curses on various acts of immorality—note that these include, but are not limited to, sexual immorality)*
- ◆ Proverbs 1.10–19 *(conspiring to theft and violence)*

- Proverbs 5.1–6 *(warnings against sexual seduction)*
- Proverbs 6.16–19 *(those actions that God hates)*
- Amos 6.4–7 *(denunciation of the rich who disregard the ruin of their neighbors).*

3. Do you think social movements should influence our reading of the Bible? Why or why not?

In what ways do you think the social movements that have insisted on equal rights for women, people of all races, and gays and lesbians have influenced or changed our reading of the Bible?

4. How have you interpreted the passages in the Bible on same-gender sexual relations that are discussed in chapter 6?

How does your interpretation affect the way you relate to homosexual individuals or same-sex couples in your congregation or community?

SESSION 5
THE ROLE OF THE BIBLE IN
OUR MORAL REASONING
Discussion of Chapter 7

Main Points
This chapter looks at some of the ways in which the Bible's moral teaching has authority in our own lives, even when in some cases it cannot be applied directly. It also offers a method for discerning how to interpret and apply the teachings of the Bible.

Questions
1. How can we separate the truly moral teachings of the Bible, applicable to all times and places, from the particular aspects of the Bible's message that are no longer relevant for us?

How can we be reasonably sure that we are not simply arranging the teachings for our convenience?

2. Using the method for discernment set forth in this chapter (pages 127–131), consider the Bible's teachings on divorce as discussed in the passages below:

+ Deuteronomy 24.1–2
+ Malachi 2.13–16
+ Matthew 5.31–32
+ Matthew 19.1–9
+ Mark 10.2–12 *(note that Mark, earlier than Matthew, gives a more rigorous rule)*
+ 1 Corinthians 7.10–16 *(note that in this passage Paul deals with marital separations as well as divorce).*

How can we develop a view of whether divorce should be allowed, and if so, under what circumstances? What factors need to be considered?

SESSION 6
THE COMMUNITY WE ARE CALLED TO BE
Discussion of Chapter 8

Main Points
The Bible describes the characteristics of the earliest Christian communities as including teaching, fellowship, worship, and care for one another. It further identifies some of these communities as places in which both Jews and Gentiles and different faith practices and models of incorporation were tolerated. Christian communities today may need to reevaluate their understanding of unity and diversity based on these biblical principles of inclusion.

Questions
1. Look up these passages from the Bible setting forth principles of life in community:

- John 13.12–20 *(wash one another's feet)*
- Ephesians 4.11–16 *(building up the body of Christ)*
- 1 Corinthians 12.27–13.13 *(the body of Christ, united in love)*
- 1 John 3.11–24 *(love one another and help the needy)*
- 1 John 4.7–12 *(love one another, for God is love).*

Based on these and other passages that come to mind, what kind of church do you think we are called to be in the world today?

How does your view of the Bible inform your understanding of Christian community?

2. How do you deal with questions of inclusion and exclusion in your congregation?

Who is placed in positions of leadership and care in your congregation, and who is excluded? Why?

3. How does the Bible encourage us to deal with conflict and difference in the church?

In what ways have you seen groups that were formerly marginalized turn around and marginalize others?

How can individuals who disagree profoundly on how to interpret the Bible live in community together?